CHILD DEVELOPMENT
(BIRTH TO ADULTHOOD)

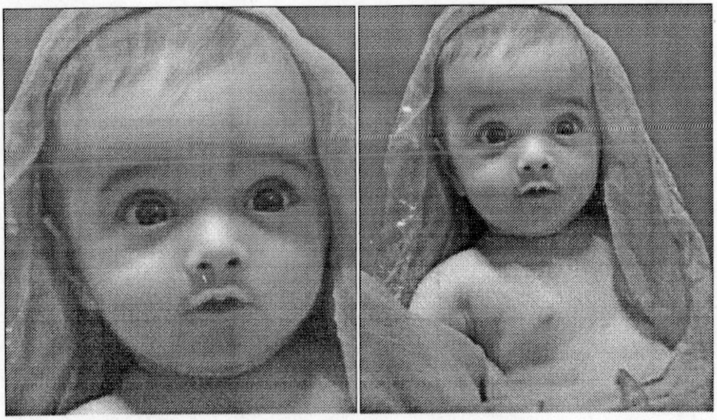

CHITRA GARG

LOTUS PRESS
4735/22, Prakash Deep Building,
Ansari Road, Daryaganj,
New Delhi - 110002

Lotus Press Publishers & Distributors
Unit No.220, 2nd Floor, 4735/22, Prakash Deep Building,
Ansari Road, Daryaganj, New Delhi- 110002
Ph:- 32903912, 23280047, 098118-38000
Email : lotuspress1984@gmail.com
Visit us : www.lotuspress.co.in

CHILD DEVELOPMENT (BIRTH TO ADULTHOOD)

ISBN : 978-81-8382-320-3

Printed & Published by : **Lotus Press Publishers & Distributors,** New Delhi- 2

CONTENTS

Child Development

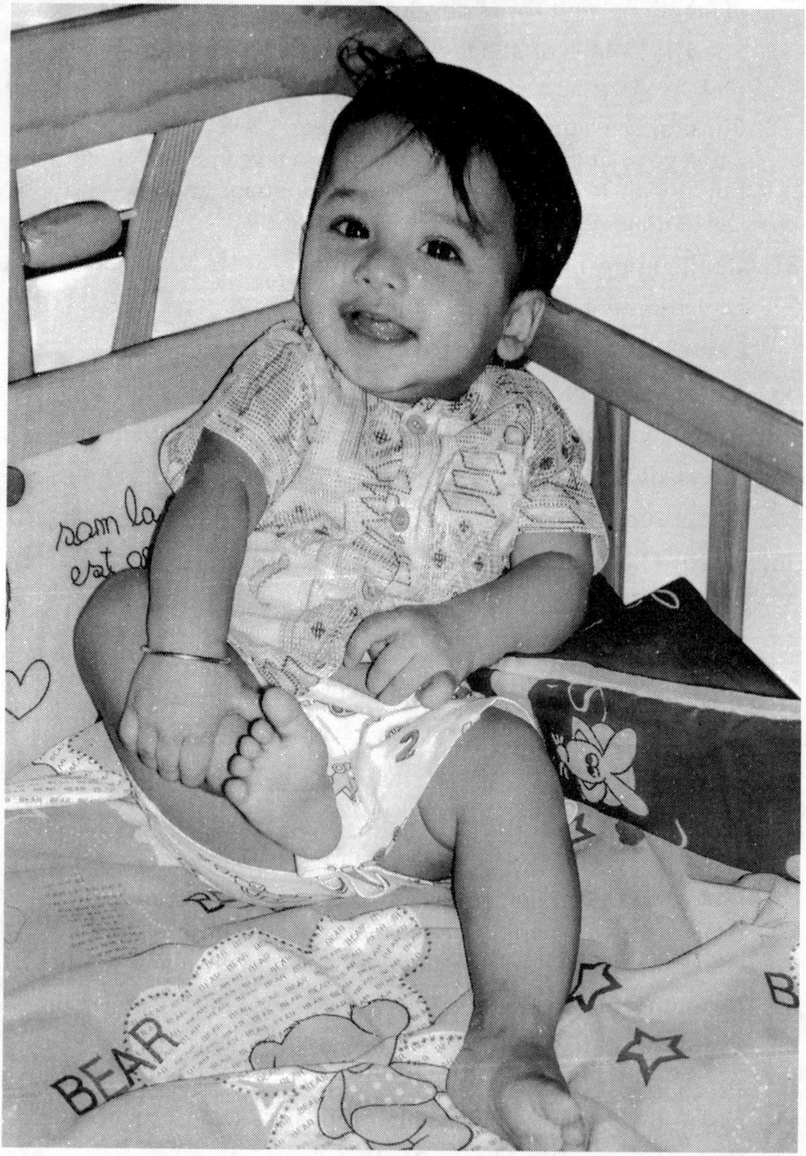

PREFACE

An Introduction to Child Development

This book deals with all the phases of child development. I have tried to give details about all round development of child. This will help all parents and teachers in better development of children.

Child development is a natural and long process. All parents are apprehensive about their growth and development. Sometimes they start worrying when they see other child's rapid growth, it may be physical or cognitive.

Child development is an extraordinary thing to observe. Any parents or anyone who cares for the kids cannot help but is fascinated by the fine growth and changes that take place from birth to young adulthood. Even young couples, who have no child, may also find this process captivating.

As the parents watch their children grow, learn and play, they may often find themselves worrying about their slow growth or fast growth or eating habits or misbehaviour. Not only parents but teachers, caretakers and therapists also have interest in the proper growth of a child. Raising a individual is really a hard work. It takes more than just waiting and worrying. It is very important to know the normal process and specific milestones of child's growth and normal development. It is also essential to understand what is abnormal. By being on the lookout for child's problems, parents can interfere and support that child needs to get back to normal life on the right track.

It is very important to remember that every child is unique. Every child develops at his/her own pace. Most of the behavior that child displays at each age and stage, his/her development is quite normal.

Parents can keep expectations about his/her abilities, behaviour, growth and developmental milestones.

The journey of child's growth is amazing. At all stages, your child needs your unconditional love and support. It is important to understand your child and his/her needs.

New born baby (from 0 to 6 months) can communicate to you only by crying. Some children cry more than others. Some children cry only when they are hungry while others can cry when their nappy is wet or not comfortable or feeling cold or hot. Give your child lots of cuddles and enjoy his/her first smile. Sometimes rocking can comfort the child.

6 to 18 months old child begins to explore the world around him/her by touching, looking, tasting and listening. Around this age, your child is curious enough and easily distracted. His/her language skill starts to develop. This may be called the '**doing stage**' of child. Your child may want to try to feed himself/herself. He/she may be fussy about food and eating habits. Tantrums are the typical behaviour at this age, so ignore them, this is normal you can feel better if you do the following things:

- You can distract the child if you can.
- You should ignore the tantrum as long as the child is safe.
- You should try to comfort the child in your easy way.
- You should involve the child in another activity.
- You should be ready to handle any situation that you can't avoid. Like you may keep his drinking water ready or keep those things ready you want the child busy with.
- You should praise the child specifically for his/her efforts of sitting, clapping, walking, standing etc.
- You should provide a safe environment.
- You should remember that the child will eat only that thing he/she likes.

- You should let the child take as much time as he/she needs to do things.
- You should not criticize or shame him/her.
- You should enjoy the activities he/she can do.
- You should not expect the child to understand things he/she is not ready for.
- You should put away precious and breakable object away from his/her reach. It is too early to teach not to touch things.
- You should expose him/her to various experiences and places.
- You should try to avoid conflict over eating. If the child has not eaten enough, keep a supply of healthy snacks and fruits when the child feels hungry.
- You should not try to teach table manner or eating habits at this age as it is too early.

Around the age between 18 month and 3 years, the child starts testing boundaries. He/she begins to understand the cause and effect of doing so. This age may be called the '**Thinking Stage**'. In this age child will be able to follow simple commands. He/she can start to think for himself/herself. The child learns to play with other children. He/she will be choosy about dress and food. Your child will be developing the concepts of past and future as well as expanding his/her knowledge of language and movement. For better development you should follow the following things:

- You should make a routine for the day and should be consistent about it.
- You should give lots of love, praise and cuddles.
- You should appreciate his/her behaviour you like most so that the child recognizes it.
- You should answer your child's questions even it he/she is repeating them. This is how your child learns.
- You should make simple and easy commands according to your child's age.

- You should encourage your child's independence in eating and doing simple things.
- You should tell rituals and stories as he/she will enjoy.
- Your child may want to eat when hungry instead of the set meal times, you should feed him/her accordingly.

Age from **3 years to 6 years** may be called the stage of **self awareness and imagination**. Around this age, child will be aware of his/her surrounding and place in the world. Throughout this stage, the child will be starting to assert his/her own identity and learning that behaviour has consequences and it has effect on others. Child will learn what he/she can control and what can't. The child will know his/her abilities. The child may live in a fantasy world and create imaginary friends. Around this stage the child develops an interest in games and rules.

For better development, you should follow these things-

- You should talk to your child about his/her feeling so that he/she can learn to express and connect his/her feelings.
- You should encourage your child to face the new challenges such as school.
- You should praise your child's good behaviour.
- You should give him/her very simple and clear commands/ instructions.
- You should answers his/her questions about life, body and world around him/her very clearly.
- You should tell your child the difference between fantasy and imagination.

—Chitra Garg
(Author)

CHAPTER 1 Baby Brings Happiness in Life

Baby is a bundle of joy for the whole family. As soon as the news spreads of conception and arrival of a baby, the whole family starts looking forward with eager and enthusiasm. A new life begins for mother and the child care begins.

It is essential that a woman who is going to conceive should be fit mentally and physically both before conception. As the baby is always demanding, mother should always be prepared to care and nurture the baby during day and night...... 24 × 7.

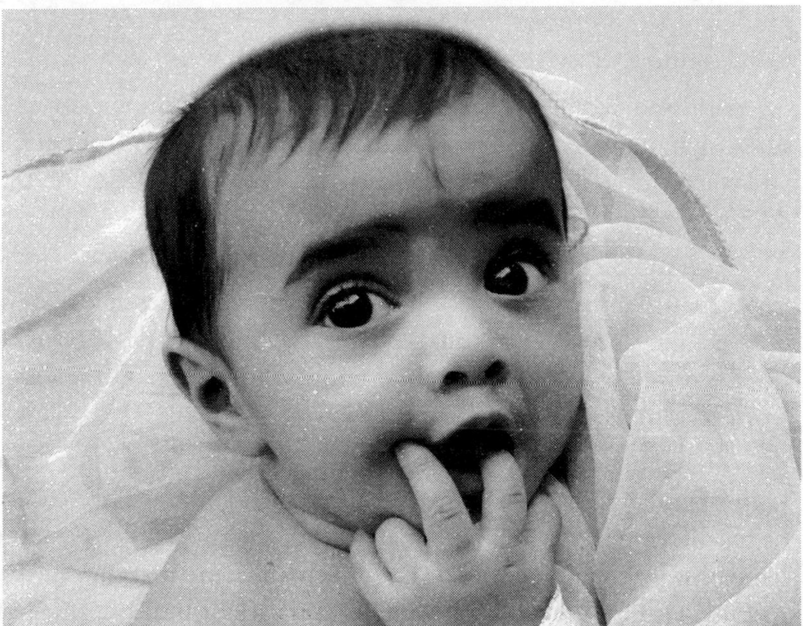

PREGNANCY

When the Pregnancy Begins

Some women don't experience any early pregnancy symptoms until the fertilized egg attaches itself to the uterine wall, several days after the conception. Generally women experience and know their pregnancy only when they miss a period. There are a few symptoms of pregnancy which women experience during pregnancy. It is not necessary that they experience them all or a few.

Signs of Pregnancy

Following are the important signs of pregnancy-

Food Cravings: During pregnancy, women feel food cravings. But sometimes it can be sign of pregnancy and sometimes not. So don't rely on this symptom. Food craving symptom is accompanied by some of the other symptoms in pregnancy.

Frequent Urination: During pregnancy once the embryo begins producing the hormone 'Human Chorionic Gonadotropin' (HCG), women find themselves going frequently to the washroom.

A missed Period: A missed period is the most important and surest sign of pregnancy. If a woman is having usually regular period and when she is late or has missed period, she should check with the doctor and have a pregnancy test.

Morning Sickness: Generally morning sickness hits the women in pregnancy until a few weeks after conception. For a couple of days or weeks they may feel nauseated and queasy. Pregnancy related nausea can hit not only in morning but at noon or night also. Some lucky women don't experience morning sickness.

Altered Sense of taste: During pregnancy women feel that their sense of taste has changed. Some feel it more than others. Their choice of food changes. They like to start eating those things they never liked or leave their favourite dish. Some women say that they have a metallic taste in their mouth while others cannot bear the smell of any particular food like Maida, flour, tea, cauliflower etc., some other women cannot tolerate the taste of coffee which they usually liked very much. This is a common sign of pregnancy.

Fatigue: This is a regular sign that women face. They feel very much tired and sometimes exhausted without any hard work. The reason for this fatigue is the high-level of the hormone progesterone that makes them feel if they have run a marathon even it they have done their normal routine work like doing work in the office or home. Fatigue is a hallmark of early pregnancy, though probably not a sure symptom on its own.

Implantation Bleeding or Cramping: After about eight days of ovulation, woman may experience implantation spotting, a slight staining of a pink or brown colour. She may feel cramping side by side. This is caused by the egg burrowing into endometrial lining. Some women might see some spotting around the time they expect their period.

Soft and Swollen Breasts: When a woman is pregnant, her breasts become increasingly tender to touch. This sign is similar to the way, she feels before her period. Once the body of the pregnant woman grows accustomed to the hormone surge, the pain will subside.

Darkening of Nipples: This may not be the sure sign of pregnancy but it is true that the skin around nipples gets darker during pregnancy. If it has started so, it means that the woman has successfully conceived. Sometimes it may be the sign of hormonal imbalance unrelated to pregnancy. Sometimes it may be a left over effect of previous pregnancy or abortion.

Important: If a woman has many of the above symptoms, she has missed her period she must take the home pregnancy test. If a blue line appears in this home pregnancy test, she is most likely on her family way. She must make an appointment with a doctor to confirm the good news.

PREGNANCY

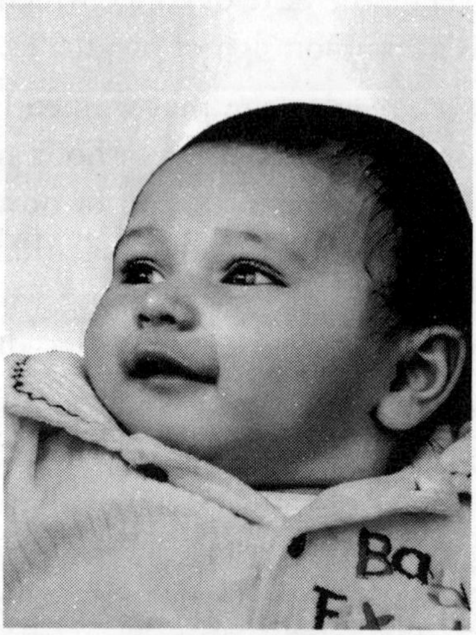

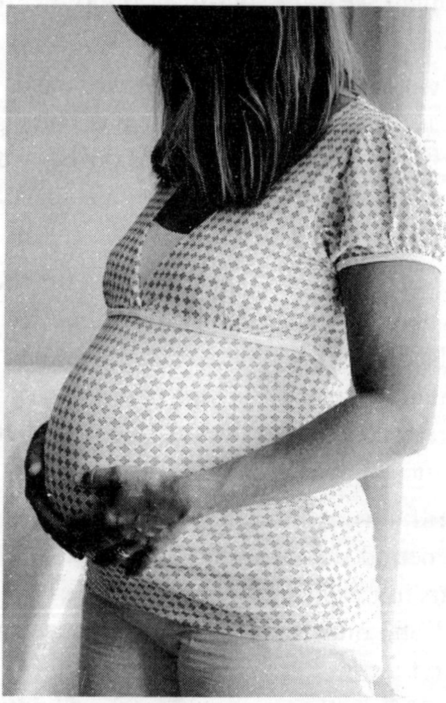

WHAT IS PREGNANCY?

Every woman needs to know what pregnancy is exactly in short. Pregnancy is the fertilization and development of one or more offspring which is known as foetus or embryo, in a woman's uterus.

An embryo is the developing offspring during the first 8 weeks following conception and subsequently the term 'foetus' is used for it until birth of child.

The pregnancy is divided into three trimester periods or we can say that there are three different stages of prenatal development. The first trimester carries the highest risk of miscarriage. During the second trimester, the development of foetus can be easily monitored and diagnosed. Then the third trimester's beginning often approximates the point of viability or the ability of the foetus to survive outside the uterus.

Childbirth usually occurs about 38 weeks after conception. The women, who have a menstrual cycle length of four weeks, take the childbirth time approximately 40 weeks. It is taken from the start of the last normal menstrual period. A lady can conceive through sexual intercourse or assisted reproductive technology.

Precautions and Care before Conceiving

- A woman, who is going to conceive, should improve her diet three months to a year before she conceives.
- She should reach her ideal weight.
- She should follow a healthy eating plan so that a normal healthy baby takes birth.
- She needs a lot of folic acid.
- She should take vitamins supplement.
- She should cut back on alcohol if she is habitual to it.
- She should cut the quantity of caffeine intake.

She should be vigilant and should try to avoid the following things:

- She should avoid sea food and fish containing mercury such as shark, sword fish and marlin. High-levels of mercury in this food can harm an unborn baby's developing nervous system.
- She should not eat more than two tuna steaks a week (weighting about 140 gm.) or four medium sizes can of tuna a week. High-levels of mercury can harm an unborn baby's developing nervous system.
- She should avoid too much vitamin A. This means she should avoid eating liver and liver products such as fish or liver oil and avoid taking supplements containing vitamin A. A pregnant woman needs some vitamin A, but if she takes it too much during pregnancy, this could harm her baby.
- She should avoid peanuts and peanut products it there is family history of allergy to peanuts, if baby's father, brother or sister have the problem of asthma, eczema. Otherwise the baby may be at higher risk of these problems.
- She must avoid unpasteurised milk and milk products. She should be vigilant about taking raw eggs and mayonnaise.
- She should avoid taking fruits and vegetable without washing them.

FOOD AND ESSENTIAL CARE EATING PLAN BEFORE AND AFTER CONCEPTION

Healthy Eating Plan

Healthy eating means a balanced diet. Her food needs to be an ideal mix of cereals, pulses, fruits, vegetables and dairy products. She should avoid foods high in fat and sugar such as cakes, sweets, biscuits and fried potato etc. She should try to eat variety of foods from all of the following groups:

1. **Cereals:** Wheat, Whole wheat bread and Pasta, Rice, Dalia, Bajra etc.
2. **Pulses:** All pulses, Sprouted Moong, Beans, Chana and Rajma.
3. **Fruits and Nuts:** Orange, Apples, Guava and dried nuts like Almonds, Cashew nuts, Walnuts etc.
4. **Vegetables:** Carrots, Spinach, Methi. Cucumber Radish and its leaves, Beet root, French Beans, Gavarfali, Lime etc.
5. **Dairy products:** Milk, Cheese, Curd, Paneer etc.

Essential Vitamins and Minerals for a pregnant woman:

A pregnant woman can take care and get essential vitamins and minerals from her food.

1. If she is vegetarian, she must ensure that her diet is not deficient in B12 and Protein. She should eat pulses daily.
2. She can get carbohydrates from bread, pasta, rice and potatoes.
3. She can get calcium from dairy foods such as milk, yogurt and cheese.
4. She should try to include soya and kootu (buckwheat) which are the plant foods that offer all essential amino acids.
5. Iron rich foods are red meat, pulses, bread, green vegetables, dried fruits and fortified breakfast cereals.
6. Small portion of fish (twice a week is enough), including some oily fish is good for pregnancy.
7. She can get proteins from foods such as lean meat, chicken, fish, eggs, pulses, beans and lentils.
8. Vitamin B12 helps to absorb iron if she takes some food or drink or fruits containing Vitamin C. A glass of any fruit juice is very useful for pregnancy.
9. She can try nibbling some Amla (Indian gooseberry) which is good source of Vitamin C and iron.

A pregnant woman should take vitamin supplement only after consulting the doctor.

Folic Acid: It is important for everyone–male or female. It helps lower the chances of heart attack, strokes, cancer and diabetes. The average Indian diet is deficient in foliates. Pregnant women are advised to increase their folic acid intake by taking a supplement. The consulting doctor helps to choose the supplement of folic acid.

In addition it is wise to eat foliate rich foods like dark green leafy vegetable–Spinach, Sarson ka saag (mustard greens), Methi (fenugreek), Citrus fruits, Whole grains, Brown Rice, Nuts, Cereals and Fortified Breads.

The following things can raise the folic acid in the body:

1. Cereals and pulses
2. Potatoes with their skin
3. Green leafy vegetables
4. Soybean and its products, soya chunks
5. Tofu
6. Almonds, walnuts, cashew nuts etc.

Fruits, Vegetables and Leafy Vegetables

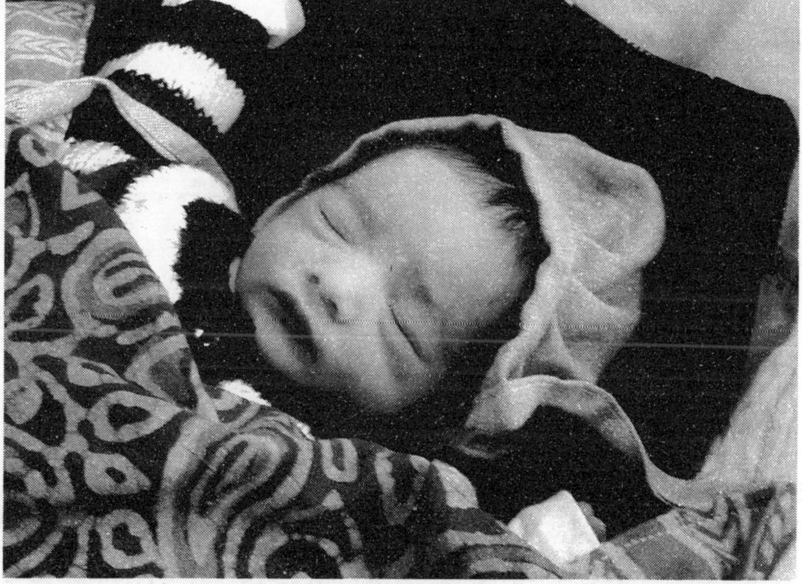

New born child needs attention and care

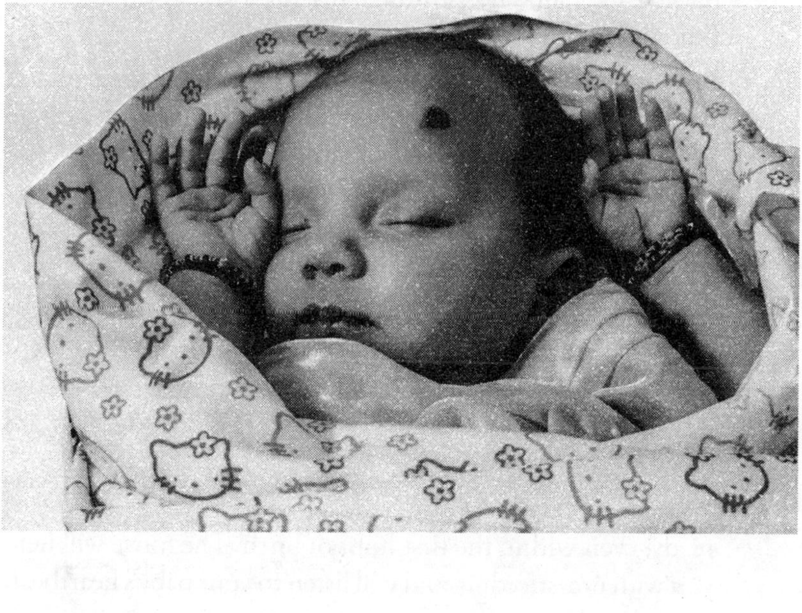

CHAPTER 2 After Delivery

Birth of Baby: Facts about New Born Baby

Just after delivery doctors and nurses will check your baby's condition at birth. Within the first hour of birth, the nurse will make sure everyone knows who your baby is by putting two name tags on him/her.

Every Mother is Eager to Know

- **How her baby looks:** Some mportant changes happen in your baby's body as he/she moves from the comfort of your womb to the outside world. As he/she cries and takes his first breaths, oxygen and blood flow through his lungs as they expand. The fluid inside them clears.
- **It's normal for your baby to look blue** in the initial few minutes after birth. Her colour will usually change from blue to pink, but her hands and feet might stay blue for a few hours or longer. The blood vessels to her/his hands and feet are very small, and it takes longer for the colour to change to pink as the blood circulates around her/his body.
- After some initial crying, **it's normal for babies to fall asleep**. But some babies might stay awake and want to feed. Because skin-to-skin contact promotes bonding and breastfeeding, it's essential at this stage.
- You can **breastfeed** your baby as soon as the baby seems ready, even within the first hour of birth. The nurse will help you with breastfeeding and will listen to your baby's heartbeat,

count breaths and take your baby's temperature regularly to make sure he/she's OK.

Child brings freshness in life

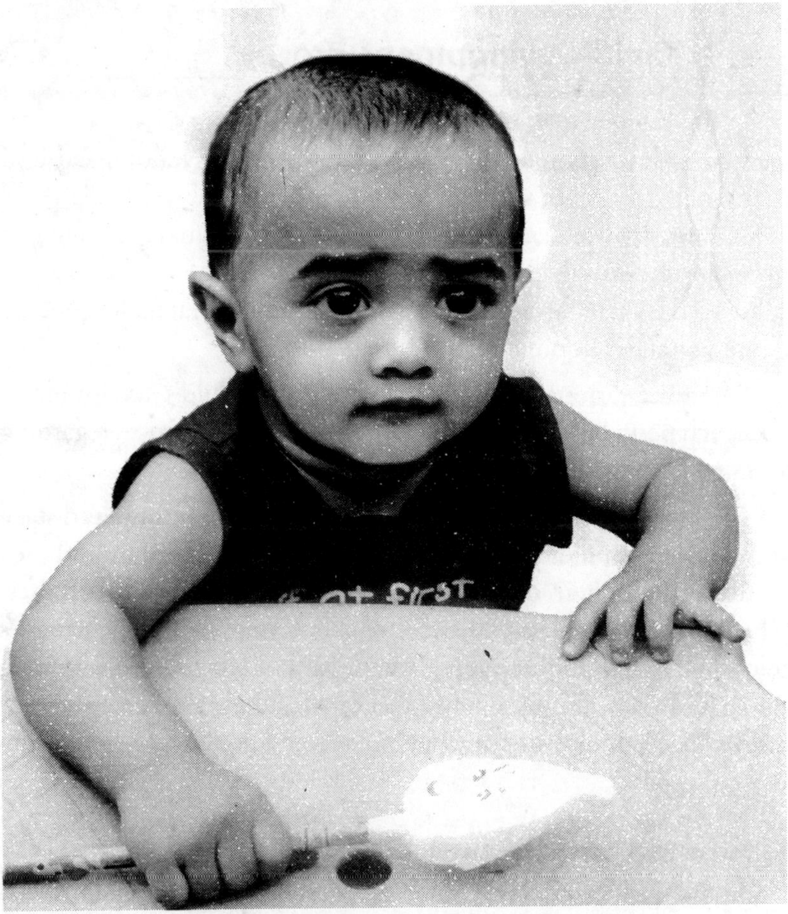

CHAPTER 3 Child Development Process

Child development means the biological, psychological and emotional changes that occur in human beings between birth and the end of adolescence. All individuals progress from dependency to increasing autonomy. These developmental changes may be strongly influenced by genetic factors and events during prenatal life, genetics and prenatal development.

There are various definitions of periods in a child's development, since each period is a continuum with individual differences regarding start and ending.

Most of the behaviour that children display at each age and stage in their development is quite normal. Every child is unique and they all develop at their own pace. Keep your expectations of their behaviour and abilities realistic, use the developmental milestones below only as a guide so you have an idea of what to expect along your child's amazing growing journey. At all ages and stages your child will need your unconditional love and support to help them along the way.

Age-Related Development Periods

Some age-related development periods and examples of defined intervals are: newborn (ages 0–4 weeks); infant (ages 4 weeks – 1 year); toddler (ages 1–3 years); preschooler (ages 4–6 years); school-aged child (ages 6–13 years); adolescent (ages 13–20). However, organizations like Zero to Three and the World Association for Infant Mental Health use the term infant as a broad category, including children from birth to age 3.

As a child develops from infant to teen to adult, he/she goes through a series of developmental stages that are important to all aspects of his/her personhood including physical, intellectual, emotional and social. The proper role of the parent is to provide encouragement, support and access to activities that enable the child to master key developmental tasks.

Parent's support and encouragement

A parent is their child's first teacher and should remain their best teacher throughout life. Functioning as a coach, the parent exposes a child to age appropriate challenges to encourage development as well as to experiences that allows the child to explore on their own and learn from interacting with their environment.

Parents need to provide the necessary support for a child to allow him to safely and productively explore and learn from his environment. Child Development experts have taken the concept of scaffolding from the building trades. Just as scaffolding is put up to support the structure of the building as it is being built and gradually taken down as the building is able to stand on its own. In the same way as the child matures and develops mastery in different fields, the scaffolding is removed or changed to allow the child to become more independent. If the child is not quite ready, the support is reinstated and then gradually withdrawn once again.

NEWBORN DEVELOPMENT

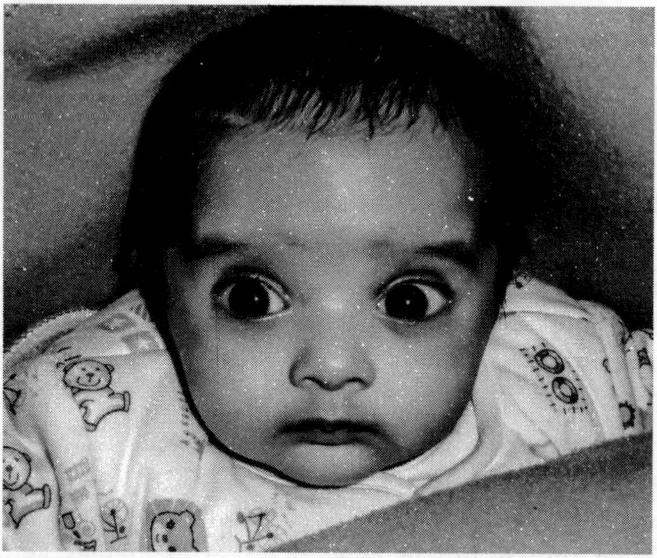

First few days

Your baby's appearance will change over the first hours and days of life. It might take a minute or two after your baby is born for his skin to become pinkish, as his lungs start to breath in oxygen. Sometimes a baby's head might be slightly cone-shaped from the birth process or there might be some marks or bruising. This will soon start to look normal.

On top of physical changes, bonding between you and your baby is one of the main areas of development in these early days.

THE FIRST WEEK DEVELOPMENT

Appearance

Your baby's appearance will change over the first week.

If your baby's head is a bit cone-shaped after her journey down the birth canal or a vacuum delivery, it'll return to normal.

Any swelling in your baby's face, including his eyelids, will go down within a few days. If your baby's face or head has been bruised – for example, after a forceps delivery – the bruising will disappear.

Your baby's umbilical cord will gradually dry, become black and then fall off, usually within the first 10 days.

Your baby might have one or more birthmarks, either at birth or developing later. Many common birthmarks **don't usually require medical evaluation**. These include Mongolian spot, Café au lait spot and Salmon patch (Stork bite). Others sometimes need checking out by a doctor, including birth mole, haemangioma and port wine stain.

Feeding and Sleeping

Your baby spends her first week of life adapting to her new environment. She needs warmth, peace, security – and lots of cuddles and holding. You can give her all of these.

Your days and nights will be dictated by your baby's cycle of sleeping and feeding. He'll sleep most of the time, waking up every few hours for a feed. It's unlikely he'll sleep through the night, especially on the first few nights of being home from hospital.

Most babies need feeds between 2-4 hours apart and have around 8-12 feeds every 24 hours. It's not uncommon for each feed to last an hour, especially if your baby's breastfeeding.

Your baby will usually wake herself when she needs to feed. But some babies might need to be woken for feeding – *for example*, babies who've lost a lot of weight, who are very small or who have jaundiced.

These are general guidelines and it's likely to be a while before you see a pattern or routine of feeding and sleeping.

Development

Your baby will close his hands involuntarily in the grasp reflex and will startle at sudden loud noises. This is very normal behaviour.

He's also likely to have sudden jerky movements while asleep. In addition to these physical developments, attachment and bonding between you and your baby is the other major area of development

Boys usually weigh more than girls and are slightly longer. There is no 'right' size for a newborn. **If your baby is active and feeding well, there's no need to worry** if the baby doesn't fit neatly into the weight-length chart you see on the baby health centre wall.

In the first nine months, your baby will roughly triple his/her weight. If the baby is **not gaining weight** at a healthy pace, it could be a feeding problem. Your elder or doctors will be able to help you sort that out.

You might not even need to use a growth chart – as your baby grows, you might notice the baby outgrowing her/his clothes, baby bath or other items that seemed enormous when she/he was a newborn.

Connection and communication with your baby

Babies often do recognise your voice. After all, your baby has been listening to you from inside your womb for the past nine months. You can communicate with your newborn using your voice, touch, sight and smell and your baby will have her own ways of telling you what she/he needs – even though she/he's not up to smiling just yet! During this first week, you'll start getting to know your baby's body language. You can hug the baby for close connection.

CHAPTER 4 Common Problems in the First Week

Sticky Eyes

It's common for babies to develop sticky or discharging eyes during the first few weeks of life. The most common cause is blocked tear ducts, and this usually gets better by itself. Gentle eye cleansing and massage will help. But it's best to have a doctor or nurse check your baby's eyes if they're sticky.

New born child's sticky eyes

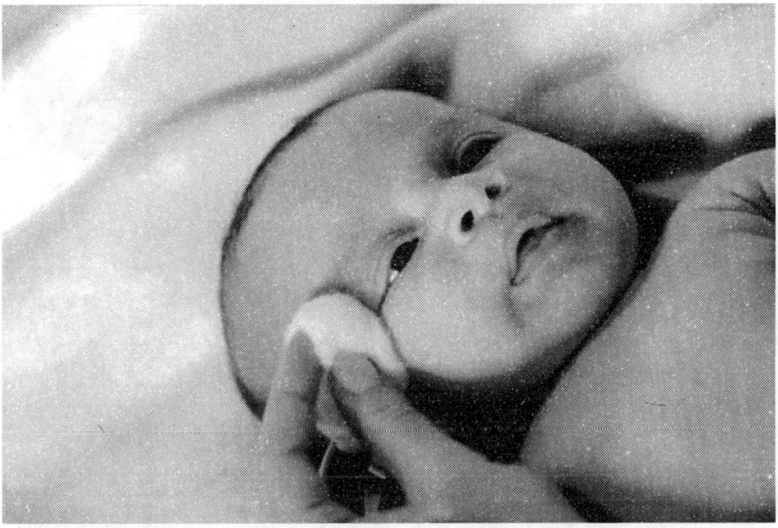

Weight loss

It's normal for your baby to lose weight during the first five days of his life, as he loses excess fluid and stool. This weight loss shouldn't be more than 10% of his birth weight, though. Most babies regain their birth weight after 1-2 weeks. If your baby has lost too much weight, you should meet the doctor to consult. Make sure that the baby is feeding enough.

Rashes

Newborn babies can develop all sorts of rashes, which usually aren't serious. But if your baby has a rash, it's best to have a doctor or nurse checks it. Common rashes include cradle cap, nappy rash, heat rash and eczema. These are sometimes due to long time dirty nappies and you don't change them immediately.

Dry skin and jaundice are other common problems for newborns. It is best to check with the doctor for the solution.

Rashes on baby hips

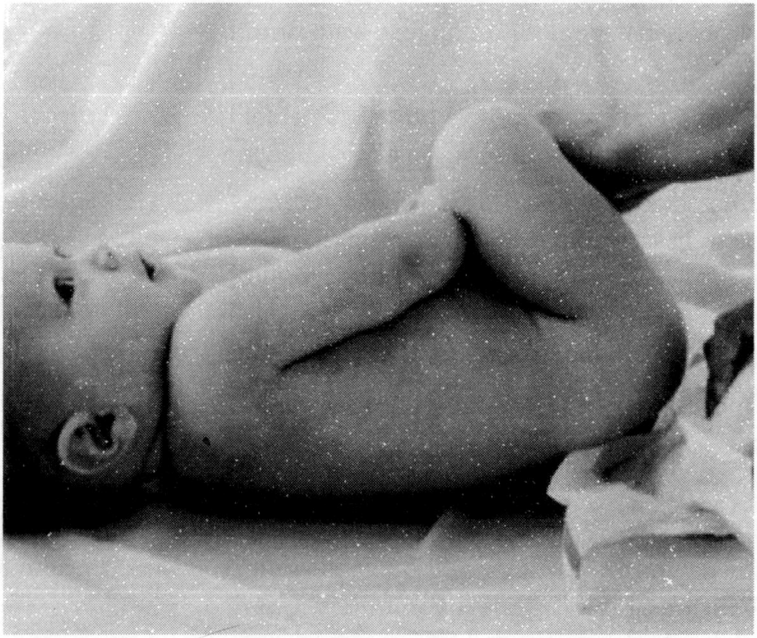

CHAPTER 5 Action and Milestone of a Baby

All babies pick up new skills in their first year . These are called milestones. Your baby might be a late starter with milestones. Don't worry.

Here's a **short guide** to some of the major milestones:

- **At birth**: Babies can't support their head unaided. They close their hands involuntarily in the grasp reflex and startle at sudden loud noises.
- **At four weeks**: Babies can focus on a face and might respond to a bell in some way (startling, crying, going quiet). They can follow an object moved in an arc about 15 cm above their faces until it's straight ahead.
- **At six weeks**: Babies might start to smile at familiar faces. They start to coo.
- **At 12 weeks**: Babies can lie on their tummies with their heads held up looking around. They can also wave a rattle, and they start to play with their own fingers and toes.

Development problem signs

It's a good idea to **have your baby checked** by your doctor if your baby:

- consistently doesn't respond to sounds
- doesn't seem to see things, has white or cloudy eyes, or there's anything about his eyes that bothers you
- can't hold his head up by 3-4 months

- continually cries for more than three hours every day, especially after 3-4 months
- doesn't move or use both arms and/or both legs
- Isn't grasping your fingers or objects.
- doesn't look at you
- isn't interested in what's going on around him
- has an unusual cry (*for example*, a high-pitched squeal

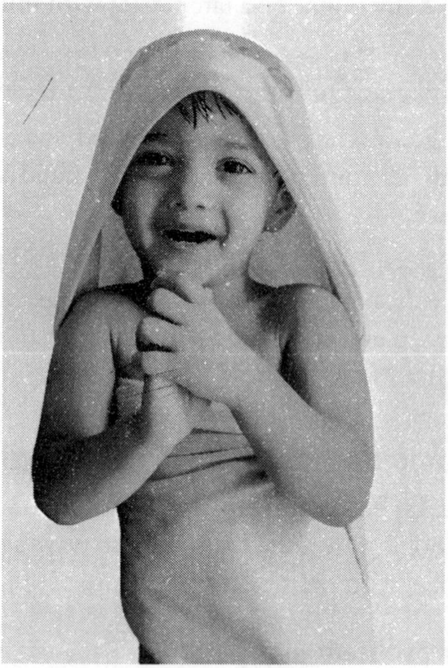

CHAPTER 6 Child's Growth Chart

Weight and Height

Age	Weight	Weight gain	Lenth/height	Height gain
At Birth	3 to 4 kg.		45-50 cm.	
1-4 Months	4 to 8 kg.	100–200 g per week	50-70 cm.	2.5 cm per month
4-8 Months	(doubling birth weight)	500 g per month	70-75 cm.	1.3 cm per month
8-12 Months	9.6 kg (21 lb) Nearly triple the birth weight by first birthday	500 g per month	Approx. 1.5 times birth length by first birthday	
12-24 Months	9–13 kg (20–29 lb)	130–250 g per month	80–90 cm (31–35 in)	5–8 cm per year
2 Years	12–15 kg (26–33 lb) about 4 times birth weight	1 kg per year	85–95 cm (33–37 in)	7–13 cm per year

Normal Heart Rate for Children

Age	Rate(Beats/Min)		
	Resting (Awake)	Resting (Sleeping)	Exercise (Fever)
Newborn	100-180	80-160	up to 220
1 week to 3 Months	100-220	80-200	up to 220
3 months to 2 years	80-150	70-120	up to 200
2 years to 10 years	70-110	60-90	up to 200
10 years to adult	55-90	50-90	up to 200

Normal Body Temperature from Infancy

Age	F Temperature C	
	Fahrenheit	Centigrade
3 months	99.4	37.5
6 months	99.5	37.5
1 year	99.7	37.7
3 years	99.0	37.0
5 years	98.6	36.8
7 years	98.3	36.7
9 years	98.1	36.7
11 years	98.0	36.7
13 years	97.8	36.6

Respiration Rate per minute for children

Age	Rate (Breaths/Minute)
Newborn	35
1 to 11 months	30
2 years	25
4 years	23
6 years	21
8 years	20
10 years	19
12 years	19
14 years	18
16 years	17
18 years	16-18

Visual Acuity Chart

Age	Visual Acuity (Snelle n Chart)
Newborn	
1 to 4 months	
4-8 months	
8-12 months	20/100
12-24 months	20/60
2 years	

Parent-child Relationship

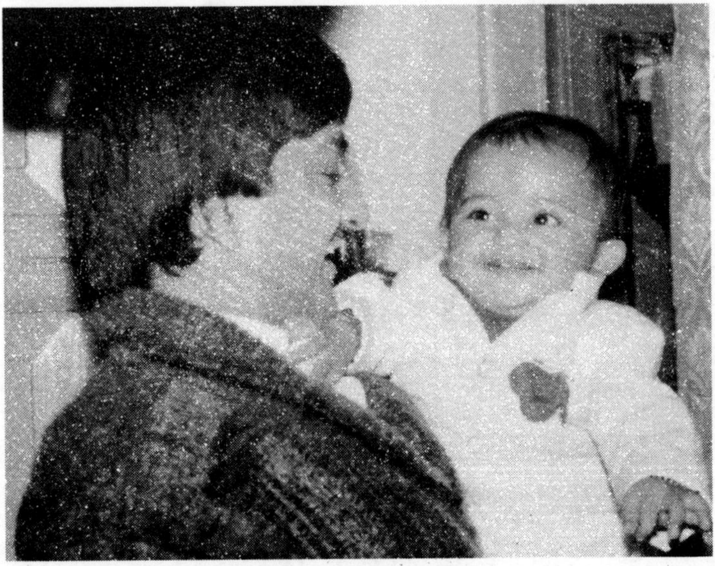

CHAPTER 7

Parent-child Relationship during Infancy-For Good Development

Parent child relationship is very important for good development of the child.

The style of attachment

Just as personalities differ in many ways, relationships differ between parent and infant. Psychologists categorize these relationships into attachment styles, which are developed through parent-child interaction. According to Carol Mooney, scholar of early childhood education and author of "Theories of Attachment," only one style, "secure attachment", can predict with high certainly that a child will have healthy relationships in adulthood. The other attachment styles tend to lead to unstable relationships in adulthood.

Activities to build a healthy relationship

Parents of infants quickly realize that there are not many complex activities, such as heart-to-heart conversations. They engage themselves for the sake of strengthening the parent-child relationship. Parents who wish to reinforce the parent-child bond should then engage in those little activities that help the child understand a parent's love. These activities include eye contact, physical contact, play, and smiling. Constant affection and showing love for a child will help stabilize the relationship and increase the likelihood that a child develops a secure attachment.

Care at stressful times

Relationship is always two-way matter. Parents of infants know how stressful having an infant in the house can be. Those little nuisances, such as crying keeping parents awake at night, are enough to drive some parents up the walls. If the annoyance of having an infant gets to a parent, the mother or father may feel like pushing the responsibility of caring for the infant at certain times to the other parent. However, parents who want to form strong parent-child bonds must push through these stressful times and give their infant the needed care, sometimes at the cost of sleep debt.

The mother's important role in new situations

At many times, the mother-child role seems more important than the father-child role. For infants, this is often the case. The mothers play the role as the "secure base" for a child. This "secure base" role shows the infant that he can be at ease in new situations, such as when strangers enter the room or when entering a new environment. Sometimes mothers may forget this duty, particularly in stressful times.

For example, when moving into a new home, moms might be busy with settling into the new house. But at this time, making the infant know he's safe in this new and sometimes scary environment is also critical. A mother who shows her child that she can be depended on will strengthen the bonds of the parent-child relationship and increase the chances that the child grow up with a secure-type attachment with family and others.

CHAPTER 8 Characteristics of the Parent-child Relationship

Whether you are expecting your first baby or the second one, you think if your parent-child relationship will be a positive one. It is completely normal thing. There are four main types of parent-child relationships: secure, avoidant, ambivalent and disorganized. Each type has its own specific characteristics. For good development of the child it is necessary to know these characteristics.

Secure relationships with parents

The secure relationship is the strongest and most positive type of attachment that a parent and child can have. The main characteristic of this type of relationship is the feeling that the child can depend on the parent. Although a securely attached child may cry when mom or dad leaves him/her at home with the other parent or grandparents or at day care or with a babysitter, the child also understands that the parent is coming back for him/her. *For example*, it's the first day of preschool and your 4-year-old throws a fit when you walk out the door. Don't fret, because after you leave, it's likely that her/his teacher will engage her in an activity and he will settle down quickly. When you return to pick him up, he gleefully greets you and may even want to stay at school for a while longer.

Avoidant relationships with parents

While the securely attached relationship shows signs of trust and reliance, an avoidant relationship often means that the child feels that he can't depend on mom or dad. Characteristics of children in an avoidant parent-child relationship often include acting overly independent, not asking parents or others for help when it is needed. They trouble interacting or playing with peers and a nonchalant or seemingly uncaring attitude when a parent leaves or returns. On the parent's side, this type of relationship is typically characterized by ignoring or disregarding the child's request for help, leaving the child to deal with his own problems or taking an overly long amount of time to respond to a child's needs or demands. Sometimes they promise something to the child, but they don't fulfil it or avoid it. If it happens many times, children don't trust the parents. This type of relationship may eventually result in much more serious effects such as depression or social withdrawal.

Disorganized Relationships

While children in ambivalent parent-child relationships may seem somewhat confused when they don't know that the parent will give them attention at that time or not, kids in disorganized attachments take this characteristic to the extreme. Children in this type of relationship act in an unpredictable manner and may have poor coping mechanisms when it comes to dealing with stress or emotional situations. Children in a disorganized relationship may have difficulty understanding other people's emotions and act in a nonsensical or confusing way. Parents in this dynamic either show little or confusing responses to the child's needs and may act neglectful.

Ambivalent Relationships

An ambivalent parent-child relationship is another negative form of attachment in which the child may exhibit insecure types of characteristics. Unlike avoidant children who tend to keep their distance from adults or act overly independent, an ambivalent attachment often results in kids who seem anxious or frustrate easily. Children in this type of dynamic may turn to their parents, looking for support or help, but then quickly turn and try to move away. Parents who exhibit ambivalent behaviours in their relationships with their children may respond in an off-and-on manner, ignoring the child at times and giving his attention at others.

THE IMPORTANCE OF PARENT-CHILD RELATIONS IN THE DEVELOPMENT OF CHILDREN

Psychologists call the relationship between child and parent as "attachment." Attachment theory, or the study of these relationships, has shed light on the importance of the relationships between parent and child as well as pointed out some of the key steps parents can take to raise their children well. In addition, mothers and fathers play different roles in bringing up a well-developed child.

Warmth of affection in parent-child relationships

The warmth of affection that parents bring to their children's lives starts at infancy. Mothers and fathers of young children shower their kids with baby-talk and physical touch. These behaviours show the child that others are sensitive of their needs and that parent can be relied on for emotional responsiveness. As a child grows older, he finds warmth in the parent-child relationship in other ways, specifically in receiving the fulfilment of his emotional needs, whether they be play or intimate conversation. Warmth in parenting can lead to a cooperative child, who is well-developed socially and emotionally.

Promoting independence

It may sound ironic but it's a fact that it is parents who lead in teaching their children; their children do not rely on their parents. Indeed, much of being a parent is teaching a child to do things for herself, from using the toilet to driving a car. One important part of this aspect of the parent-child relationship is disciplining children, which often is a way of keeping children on track in their own initiatives. Setting limits, such as restricting the amount of television time per day, helps children stay focused on their own responsibilities, such as finishing homework.

The importance of Mother and Father in development

Moms and dads play different roles in the development of a child. The differences can be roughly summed up in the following way: Moms are protectors and educators; dads are life coaches and counsellors. Moms act as a safe base on which children can rely; they teach their children not to be afraid of new surroundings. Moreover, according to researchers as moms tend to spend more time engaging in low-intensity activities, such as reading and game-playing, with their children, children begin to see mothers as teachers. The father's role in a child's development has traditionally been underestimated. The fathers play an integral role in the emotional and social development of children. Father-child interaction tends to be more intense, and through their shared activities children learn how to express and control their emotions with their fathers. By working together, mothers and fathers help their children develop their skills across the spectrum.

Teaching the child

From early childhood, the home becomes a school for the children. To parents of older children, this is obvious, as after dinner the dinner table might become the family study table. However, parents' roles in educating young children start as early as the toddler years. Parents simultaneously educate their children while they strengthen the parent-child attachment. For example, reading books to your child will strengthen his linguistic development. Playing active games with your child will improve his motor skill development and finishing puzzles with your child will enhance his cognitive development. Young children and their parents might mistakenly believe they are just spending quality time with family when they are actually developing useful life skills.

CHAPTER 9

Positive Parenting brings Positive Development in Children

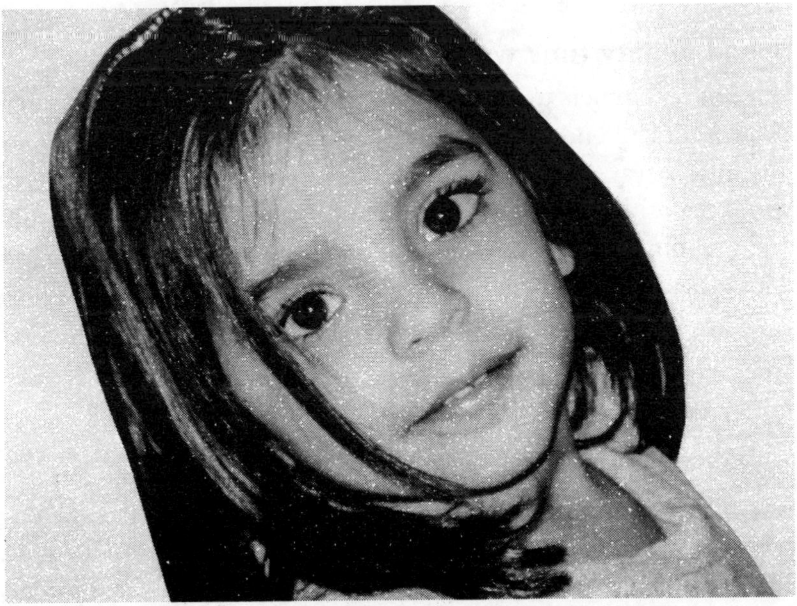

Children raised in loving homes often thrive and do the best in their fields. When parents focus on their child's needs, show that they love and value their child and strive to be good role models, they are implementing positive parenting skills. Positive parenting effectively helps children to develop a secure attachment between parent and child and nurtures a sense of positive self-worth.

Create Self-Esteem in children

You must realise how important a child's self-esteem is since it becomes his arm or for facing life's challenges. By praising your child for his efforts and not just the result, you are helping him develop a strong sense of self-worth and teaching him to overcome disappointments. Remember, too, that you are very much influential regarding your child's behaviours. If you model a positive, realistic attitude about your own strengths and weaknesses for him, the child would emulate as he grows and develops.

Spend quality time with the child

The researchers urge parents to spend time each day with their child. Your child needs attention and when he doesn't have it he may act up as a way of getting you to take notice. Allow your child to connect positively with you by having meals together as a family, and spending time reading books or playing board games together. This focus and attention encourages contentment in your child, which often leads to the development of good behaviours and a strong sense of security in him/her.

Teach discipline in life

Dr. Seema Malhotra shares her belief that by disciplining in a way that allows children to experience responsibility that is directly related to their privileges, a child will become capable and accountable. Doctors encourage an authoritative style of parenting, where parents and children work together to come up with rules that benefit one another. In this style of parenting, the parent is kind and respectful yet firm when disciplining, which also encourages a healthy attachment between parent and child.

Encourage Friendships and teach to resolve problems

You are giving him the opportunity to create friendships by hosting play dates and scheduling outings with your child and his peers, and you're encouraging positive social development. He begins to understand the value of friendship and he learns important social skills such as sharing and taking turns. When he has a disagreement with his friends, your intervention helps train him to resolve conflict in a positive way, without resorting to aggressive behaviour.

Spend time with children

CHAPTER 10 Important Things that Affect Child Development

Early childhood is one of the most important stages of a person's life. Children during this phase of development grow rapidly, both physically and cognitively. There are a wide range of issues that affect this vital time. The World Health Organization estimates that more than 200 million children fail to meet their full potential because many of their most basic needs aren't met. Parents, caregivers and community leaders have the opportunity to make a difference in young children's lives.

Several factors contribute to your child's development in the early years. As a parent, you have a vital role in shaping your little one's experiences and assisting him/her in reaching her full potential. Help your child succeed by becoming an informed and active participant in his/ her life.

Calm and safe environment

Providing a safe, clean, calm and comforting environment is essential for your child's development. Keep hazardous and inappropriate toys away from young children. An environment where your child is exposed to physical or verbal abuse will negatively affect his development. Not only is your child missing out on seeing what a healthy relationship looks like. Stressful situations cause the body to release elevated levels of the stress hormone cortical. Extended periods of this hormone can make the brain vulnerable to processes that can destroy brain cells or lower the number of connections in the brain.

Good Nutrition

Your child needs adequate nutrition to allow his body and mind to develop properly. Feed your child those foods that are appropriate for his age. Breast milk or formula can provide almost every nutrient a baby needs for the first months of life. As a child grows, his nutrition needs change. Your paediatrician can help guide you on what foods are best at each stage. Fruits, veggies, whole grains, lean meats and water are all part of a well-balanced diet as your child gets older. Malnutrition can lead to development issues and a failure to thrive.

According to the World Health Organization, up to 25 percent of children in developing nations lack basic nutrition and even in developed nations, children suffer from malnutrition. Lack of healthy food leads to stunted physical growth, slowed or reduced brain development and the suppression of the immune system. This leaves these little ones at risk for viral, bacterial and parasitic infections. Simply stated, children whose early childhood is marked by malnutrition face a lifetime of health issues. The good news is that these can all be avoided by making a variety of healthy foods and supplemental vitamins available to children.

Parental involvement is required

As one of the strongest influences in your child's life, you can help him develop to his full potential. Be sensitive to your child's needs and respond quickly. Don't be afraid to show your child affection by hugging, kissing and snuggling with him. Use kind words and a warm tone. Laugh, play, dance and sing with your child as much as you can. Nurture and love your child to help him develop through these vital years. According to **Dr. S. Sethi**, positive stimulation from the time of birth is a crucial factor in children's development for a lifetime.

Stimulation

According to the researches, the amount of stimulation provided in a child's environment can dramatically affect her brain and cognitive development. W.H.O. states that this is especially important during the first 3 years of life because early childhood is the most intensive period of brain development during a person's life. Hands-on experiences, such as touching a cat, grasping a spoon, rolling a ball or handling various types of cloth do wonders for your child's brain development. Show him how to properly touch, listen, talk, play, smell, look and hear the world around him. This world is new to him, so let him make those connections.

Healthcare of children

Doctors do more than just help young children get over the sniffles. Adequate healthcare during the critical years of early development can identify and help to fix health and developmental issues before they become critical. The pae-diatricians can help parents by teaching parents as to what to look for and how to identify key developmental stages.

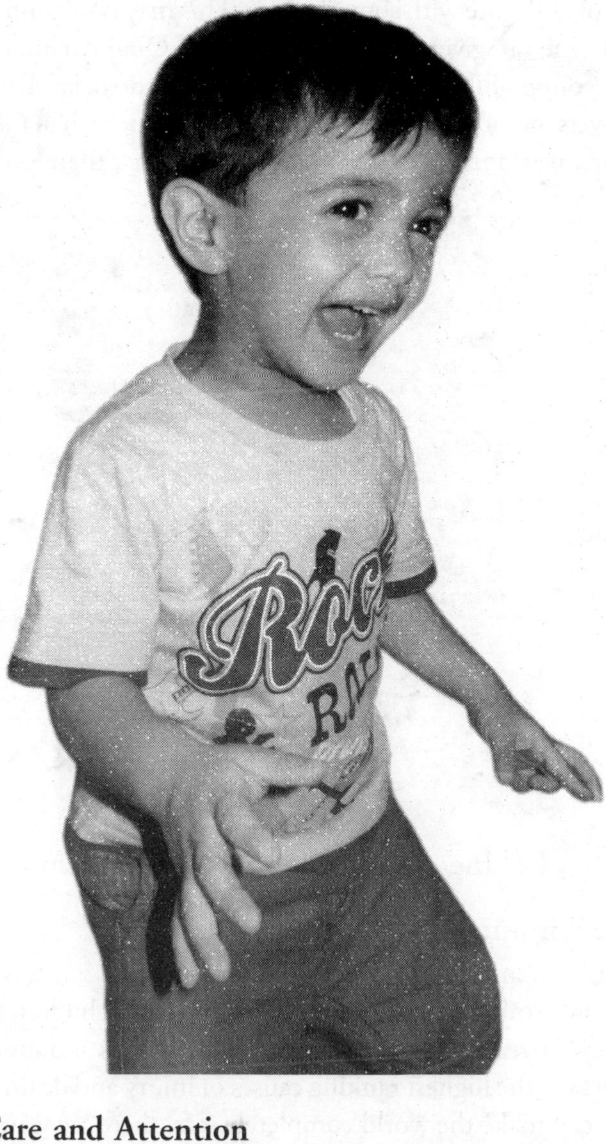

Child Care and Attention

In a perfect world, every child would get the undivided attention of a parent until he is ready to start to go to school. But the reality is far different. Half of all parents with children a year old share the duties of childcare with someone else. This may be a family member, an in-home caregiver or a childcare centre. Quality childcare is vital to the young child's physical, intellectual and social development. Caregivers for infants should have a ratio of no more than three infants, and caregivers for toddlers should have no more than four children.

Let the child try to do thing and enjoy

Safe environment

To learn and grow properly, children need a safe environment. It's an unfortunate fact that thousands of young children are hurt or killed every year. There are lists of accidental falls and motor vehicle accidents as the highest ranking causes of injury and death. While no parent can make the world completely safe, there are ways to tip the odds in the child's favour. It is vital that parents educate themselves on safety issues, including the proper use of car seats, household and environmental safety.

Parental Bond

Relationship of Children with Peers
and Grandparents is Important

CHAPTER 11 Various Relationship Affect Child Development

Personal relationships and social bonds with parents and peers can have significant effects on a child's development. Depending on the quality of these relationships, the development can be either positive or negative. Given the importance of personal relationships on child development, parents can play an important role in their child's growth by fostering healthy, positive interactions in all domains of the child's life.

Parental bonds with child

A child's bond with his parent or caretaker is one of the most important factors affecting her/his development. Early parental bonds establish a child's attachment patterns, which affect his interactions not only during childhood, but throughout his entire life. A child who grows up with little physical contact or sense that her parents are going to meet his physical and emotional needs may grow up to be anxious, apprehensive to interact with others or may display physical aggression.

Parent's behaviour with others

A parent's personal relationships with her spouse or friends can also affect a child's development. If a child grows up witnessing his parents handle interpersonal conflicts through yelling, passive-aggressive comments or aggressive behaviours, she or he may model these interactions in his/her own life. Further, in situations where a child witnesses domestic violence, she or he may experience persistent negative effects, even if the child witnesses the violence when she or he is very young. Early exposure to domestic violence can create permanent changes to the brain that affect children's learning and development.

Social relationships of children with peers

Once a child begins to form his own social relationships, they can affect his development, particularly during the teenage years. During adolescence, peers' perceptions of young people can have a strong effect on their self-image and their emotional development. Further, acceptance by peer groups and friends can affect a child's concept of how he fits in with society. His confidence can shape his plans for the future and overall psychosocial development.

Relationships with Society and the Community

The community environment can also affect a child's development. Specifically, the larger community also contributes to the child's developmental outcomes through its availability of resources and the cultural milieu. Access to educational and mental health services as well as community supports for parents can have strong effects on whether a family is able to meet their child's basic needs.

CHAPTER 12 Maternal Behaviour and Employment Affect Child Development

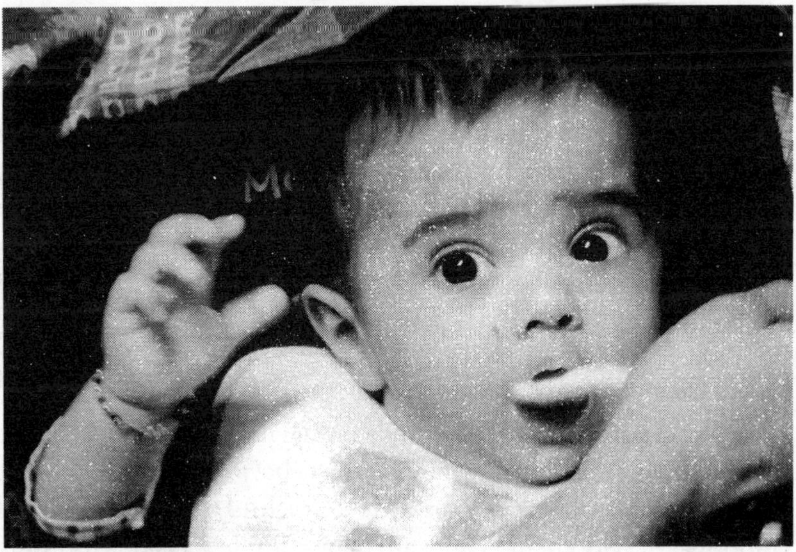

Most common factors

There's no doubt that mothers have a huge impact on how their children develop. Some behaviour plays a bigger role in how your child turns out. Some of them are positive and others not so much, but if you understand how they contribute to gains or delays in development, you'll be better able to stick with the good behaviours and refrain from the bad ones. But remember you don't have to worry about your all activities and little things you do.

Working mothers

Maternal employment rates have risen dramatically over the last 25 years. While there is evidence that the development of children may be altered by the absence of their mother during work hours, there are additional variables that contribute to this effect. The number of hours worked, the type of work schedule, when a woman returns to the work force and even racial variables may all affect the way development pans out in children of working mothers.

There's no way around to earn money and to take care of your kids, especially if you're in need of money for your family. Children of women who work full time suffer mild setbacks in terms of cognitive development. The effects occur all the way into first grade, but the same children benefit from a working mother because their household income is higher. This means mothers have access to better child care and schools. The study found that working mothers were also more responsive to their children when they were together than stay-at-home mothers.

Expression of Love and Affection

Mothers usually have no trouble displaying how much they love their children. It turns out that the loving behaviour has a large impact on your child. Affection toward your child boosts brain and emotional development. There are many simple ways of expressing love and affection like cuddling and kissing a young child and hugging, giving a high five or putting your arms around an older child. Reading, singing, playing, bathing, eating together, watching movies, taking a walk or just spending time together are other easy ways to show your child that you love him while helping him develop cognitively and socially.

Feeding variety of Food

Kids need to eat, but not just anything will do. Children's bodies and brains develop optimally when they get a well-balanced and varied diet made up of foods from different food groups. Doctors recommend breastfeeding your baby as long as possible for a healthy start to life. Once your child moves to big kid, foods, fruits, vegetables, dairy foods, protein and whole grains, provide his body with the nutrients, he needs to grow healthy bones, muscles, organs, eyes and brain. This ensures normal cognitive and physical growth.

Risky Behaviour and Bad habits

Keeping your child safe is one of your primary jobs as a mother. However, if you engage in risky behaviour, you increase the risk that your child might too do the same. *For example*, smoking or eating tobacco in front of your child sends the message that it's okay. Even if your child never picks up a cigarette, breathing in second-hand smoke can interfere with development as well. Regular exposure can lead to issues with learning and behaviour. Other risky behaviour, such as substance abuse, can interfere with your ability to keep your child safe and healthy, which can delay his development.

Stages of Child Development

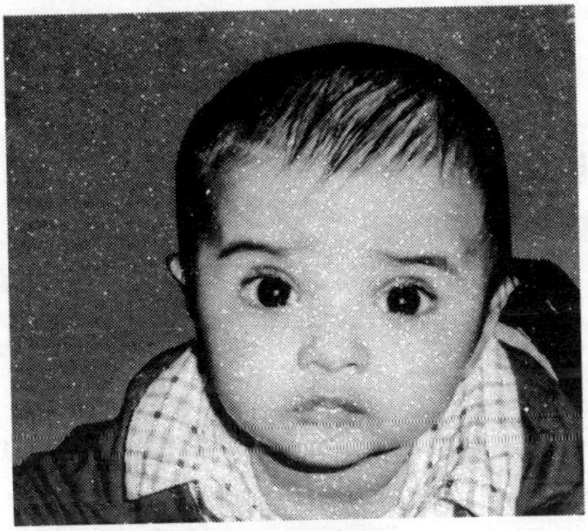

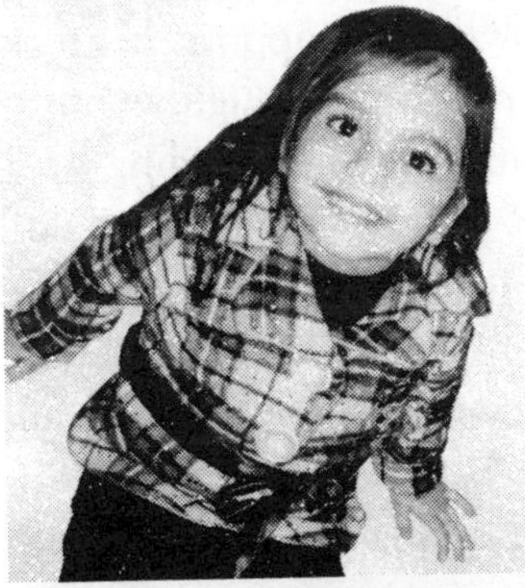
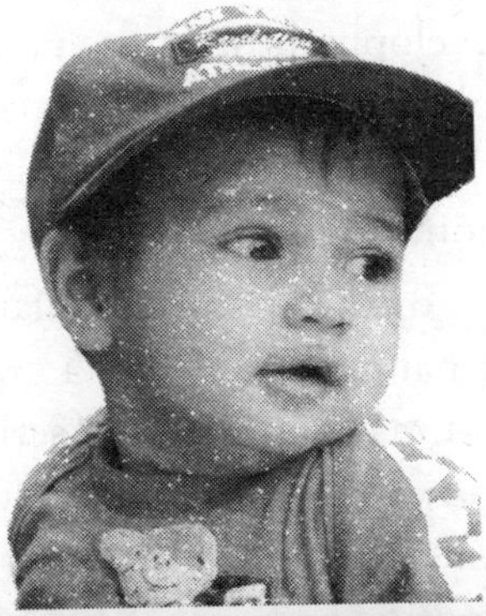
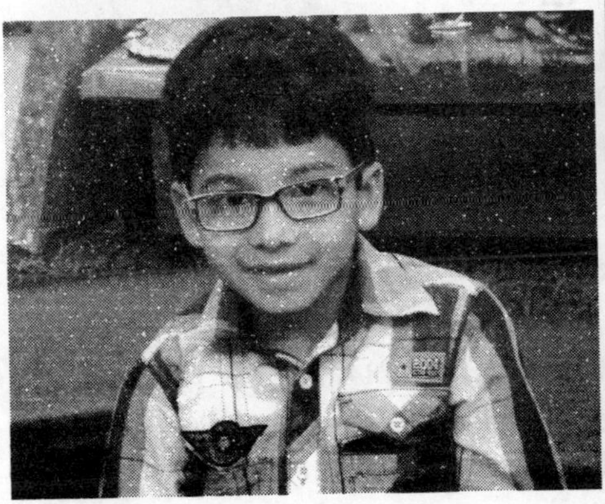

CHAPTER 13 Stages of Child Development from Infancy to Adolescence

Infancy (New born to 1 year)

Lot of changes occur during this infant period. During the first year of your child's life, he will go from a naive newborn that has little motor control to toddling baby. This first stage of child development includes rapid physical growth that supports her new abilities. Major milestones include rolling over at roughly 4 to 6 months, sitting up unassisted by 6 months old and crawling by 8 months and even walking by 12 months.

By the end of the infant stage children also have the fine motor, or hand, skills to use a grasp, pick up and put down small objects and make attempts to scribble with a crayon or other writing tool. You will also notice, as your child reaches between 4 and 6 months, that he will begin to purposefully babble and laugh or squeal with emotion.

By 12 months old, an infant may also have the ability to say simple words, such as "mama," and understand a limited vocabulary of basics, such as "yes" or "no" or "come". His weight increases three times to birth weight.

Toddlers (1 year to 3 years)

In the toddlers age group between 1 and 3 years old, your child makes major strides toward independence. During the toddler stage, children are up on their feet walking and running. By 24 months, most children can kick a ball, walk up and down stairs with help and carry objects while moving.

Toddlers can also scribble, making marks that they see as real objects, build block towers and start to feed themselves. Toddlers language and communication skills sharply increase at this stage, with the typical 2 year old understanding between 500 and 700 words and speaking well over 500 words.

Toddlers are immature, socially and emotionally, having little self-control and an unsophisticated style when "playing" with peers. *For example*, it is very common for a toddler to hit or yell when trying to share a toy with another child of his age.

Preschool children (4 years to 5 years)

Even if your child doesn't attend a formal preschool program, the ages between 3 and 5 are typically known as the preschool stage. By age 4, most children can move well, hopping and standing on one foot, kicking a softball with ease and even throwing a ball overhand.

By 5 years old, children may even climb on play equipment, somersault and skip. Additionally, the preschooler's growing fine motor and cognitive skills allow him draw geometric shapes, patterns and human figures and write some letters of the alphabet. Emotionally, the preschooler is building greater self-regulation abilities and has the ability to verbally express what he is feeling instead of only using gestures or physical aggression.

If you observe socially, preschoolers are entering a new world where they are making their first true friends based on similar interests. They have the skills to share and take turns and can show empathy toward others.

School Children (6 years to 12 years)

From approximately age 6 to early adolescence, children are most often known as grade scholars or school children. At this stage, like the name says, children enter grade school. During the early grade school years, children may rely more on parents for their emotional and social needs.

As the child moves through these years toward adolescence, peers factor in more and play larger roles in the child's life. Physically, the school child has the gross motor abilities to tackle new forms of movement, such as sports or dance lessons, as well as fine motor skills that allow for realistic drawing and writing of the alphabet. School children are also taking on more of an academic role and learn educational basics that they will use throughout their life, such as mathematics, language, writing and science.

Adolescence (13 years to 17years)

In our country some children at the age of thirteen look like small children, while some others especially girls show many physical and attitude changes.

The teen years mark the major departure in development, as the child begins to look and act more like an adult than a little kid. During the beginning of adolescence, children will go through a set of physical changes known as puberty. This includes the onset on menstruation, developing body hair and in boys a voice change. Teens typically strive to become more independent and often focus more on friendships and romantic relationships than those with their immediate family. Additionally, some adolescents may look toward their adult futures and investigate a potential profession through internships or after-school jobs. The development speed at this age depends more on environment. In metropolitan cities or in rich families, adolescents grow rapidly and make visible changes in their thoughts and physique.

CHAPTER

14 Types of Child Development

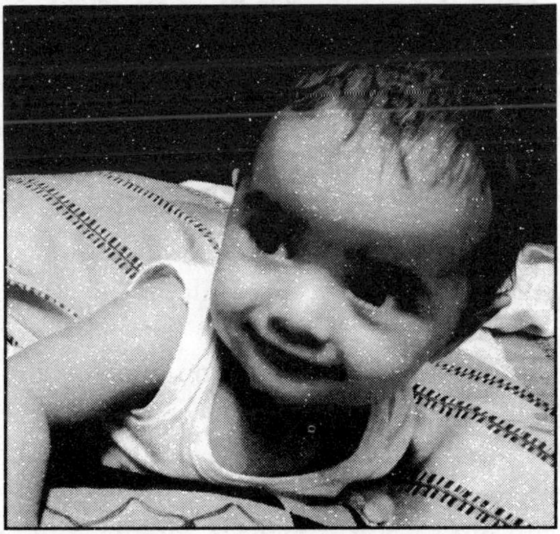

As a parent, it's normal to worry about whether your child is developing appropriately or not, especially if he seems to be lagging compared to other children. Development happens in a unique way for each child, but learning to recognize behaviours associated with developmental stages could aid in early detection. **Three typical stages of development are physical, psychosocial and cognitive.** Knowing about these stages is important as well as necessary'.

Physical Development Stage

Physical development refers to changes in the growth and function of the body. Over months and years, a child should display physical characteristic appropriately, indicating his development is on track. Detection of abnormalities or delays in development at this early age may result in more effective treatment options. Pay attention to your child's eye movements, muscle development and auditory responses. Monitoring your child's abilities to respond to changes in lighting and scenery, bring a spoon to her mouth or hear someone clap, will assure you that his physical development is on track. *For example*, from infancy to 2 years of age, your little one is quickly adjusting to the new experiences of the "outside" world

Psychosocial Development Stage

Child's psychosocial development begins at infancy, shaping whether your child views the world as a safe place where he belongs. At each age, the presence of specific characteristics in your child indicates healthy development. Your child begins asking questions with broader concepts, while having the expectation that he be given detailed answers. It is particularly important to positively support your child during this time, as the new social experiences often bring about feelings of insecurity and anxiety, which may affect self-esteem. *For example*, children ages 6 to 12 years, school aged children, have more opportunities for socializing outside the family unit and must learn to manage emotional responses in an acceptable way.

Cognitive Development Stage

Cognitive development is the bridge between physical and mental function of a child. It can be monitored, like physical development, by comparing your child's behaviours to the expected abilities for his age group. *For example*, at ages 3 to 5 years your child will begin to retain simple information, allowing him to learn and remember some of the colours, alphabet and numbers. This is the period during which he will begin understanding rules — both the rules of his parents and his environment — with the ability to talk about these rules in fragmented or full sentences. For example, your child might make statements such as "Don't touch … hot or good." It is through cognitive development that your child will grow to understand, and operate successfully within, his environment.

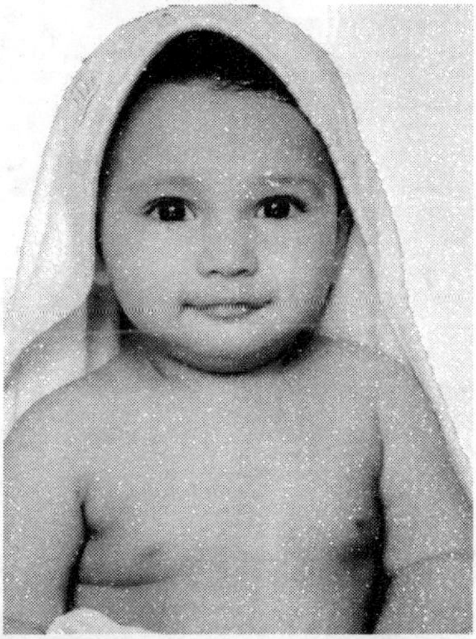

CHAPTER 15 Specific Physical Developments and Changes

1 to 4 months

- Infant's head and chest circumference are nearly equal to the part of the abdomen.
- Head circumference increases approximately 2 cm per month until two months, then increases 1.5 cm per month until four months. This Increase is an important indication of continued brain growth.
- Continues to breathe using abdominal muscles.
- Skin remains sensitive and easily irritated.
- Gums are red.
- Eyes begin moving together in unison.
- Cries with tears.

4–8 months

- Head and chest circumferences are basically equal.
- Head circumference increases approximately 1 cm per month until six to seven months, then 0.5 cm per month; head circumference should continue to increase steadily, indicating healthy, ongoing brain growth.
- Breathing is abdominal. Respiration rate depends on activity. Rate and patterns vary from infant to infant.
- True eye colour is established.
- Baby Fat appears on thighs, upper arms and neck in some infants.
- Teeth may begin to appear, with lower incisors coming in first. Gums may become red and swollen, accompanied by increased drooling, chewing, biting and mouthing of objects whichever come in his/her hands .
- Legs may appear bowed; bowing gradually disappears as infant grows older.

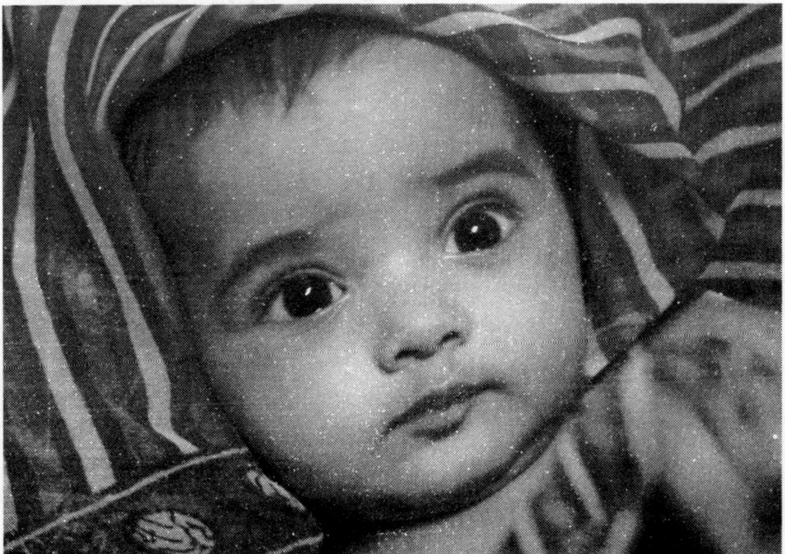

8–12 months

- Head and chest circumference remain equal.
- Continues to use abdominal muscles for breathing.
- In this age group, respiration rates vary with activity.
- Environmental conditions, weather, activity and clothing still affect variations in body temperature.
- More teeth appear, often in the order of two lower incisors then two upper incisors followed by four more incisors and two lower molars but some babies may still be waiting for their first.
- Both eyes work in unison.
- Can see distant objects and points at them.
- Arm and hands are more developed than feet and legs, sometimes hands appear large in proportion to other body parts.
- Legs may continue to appear bowed.
- Feet appear flat as arch has not yet fully developed.
- "Baby Fat" continues to appear on thighs, upper arms and neck.

Toddlers (1 to 2 Years)

- Head size increases slowly; grows approximately 1.3 cm every six months; anterior fontanel is nearly closed at eighteen months as bones of the skull thicken.
- Weight is now approximately 3 times the child's birth weight.
- Rate of growth slows a little bit.
- Toddler's respiration rate varies with emotional state and activity.
- Chest circumference is larger than head circumference in toddlers.

- Toddler will begin to lose the "Baby Fat" once he/she begins walking.
- Legs may still appear bowed.
- Body shape changes; takes on more adult-like appearance; still appears top-heavy; abdomen protrudes, back is swayed.

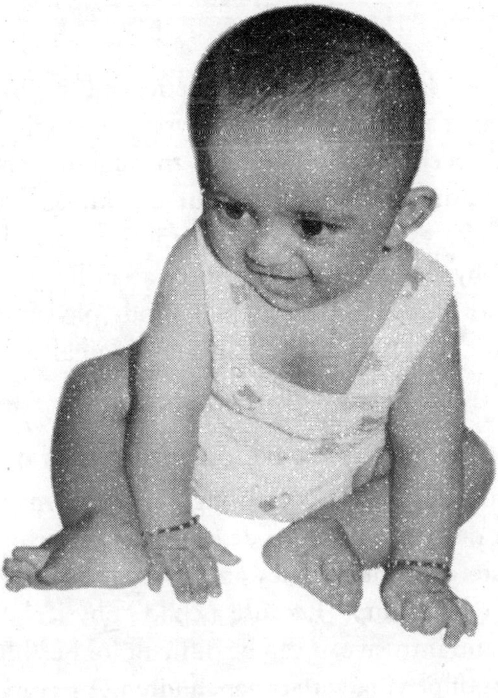

CHAPTER 16 How Physical Development Influences Child's Emotional Development?

At times we see that children experience fast physical changes than others. It is a common thing. Physical, mental and emotional development occurs simultaneously throughout childhood and adolescence. Emotional development encompasses how a child experiences, expresses and manages emotions and her ability to establish healthy relationships with others, according to the California Department of Education. As a child's body physically changes, it can influence whether healthy psychological and emotional development takes place.

Impact of physical and learning disabilities on child

Children with physical or learning disabilities may be at risk for unhealthy or delayed emotional development. Learning disabilities can exacerbate emotional issues and prevent the development of healthy peer relationships. Because a child's physical disabilities are more visible and intrusive, it can be difficult for her/him to gain the social benefits of playing with other children. A research report says that children with disabilities may be slower to develop emotions and weaker in expressing those emotions, and may have difficulty forming attachments, which impacts identity development.

Childhood obesity and emotional development

Childhood obesity is more prevalent than ever before in society. There are strong implications and problems not only for a child's physical health, but psychological development as well. Social discrimination and low self-esteem are common issues for overweight or obese children. Specialist can help to improve the treatment of child psychiatric disorders through scientific practice, research, and education. Because of the societal pressures surrounding the "ideal" body type, overweight or obese role in children are at higher risk for developing eating disorders or suffering from an unhealthy body image. Parents should take notice of this development and try to help the child in the best way.

Parent's Role in fostering healthy emotional development

Parents who actively and intentionally play a part in all areas of their child's life can foster healthy physical, mental and emotional development. Interacting directly and participating actively in discipline, and emotionally identifying and helping a child connect with family history can positively impact psychological and emotional development. When parents have a healthy relationship with their child, the negative impact of disabilities, obesity or other physical issues on emotional development can be minimized. This is parent's moral duty to foster healthy emotional development of the child.

Monitoring child development and resources

If you notice that your child is not responding as expected, speak with your doctor to find out if a medical issue is present. If you are curious to find out more specific details about the many milestones your child will achieve over the months and years to come, there are very good resources available. You can also consult your doctor, clinics and child care centres, which typically offer additional resources.

Role of Play in Child Development

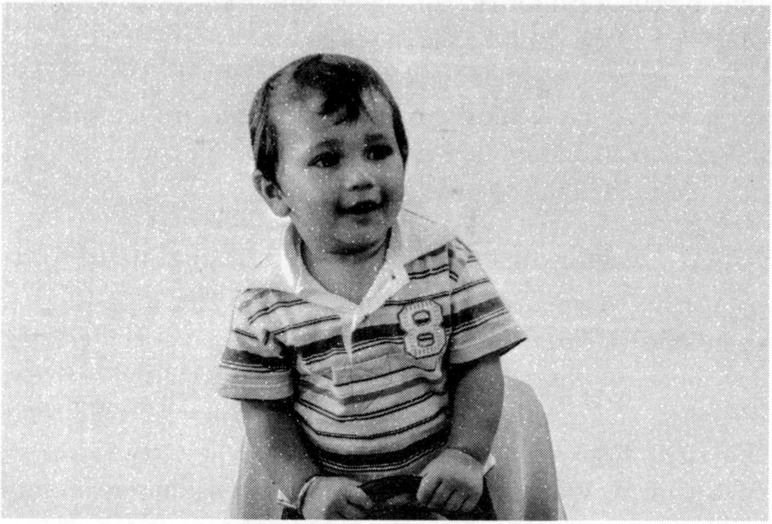

Every child likes to play in his own way

CHAPTER 17 Role of Play in Child Development

Every child likes to play. But each child has different method of playing. Play is a vital part of child development, but children of different ages do not play in the same way. This is because play occurs in stages that reflect where children are socially, cognitively and emotionally at different ages. Your child may reach each stage before or after other children in his age group, but this is normal because every child is different and develops at their own rate.

There are different child behaviours while playing. Some of them are following:

Observant children (till 12 months)

According to Abhie Paren-ting, infants engage in what's called "onlooker" or "obser-vant" play up to about 12 months of age. They prefer to sit on your lap and watch other children at play, rather than engage in the play themselves. Infants are fascinated by those around them, and learn who they can rely on to feed, entertain and soothe them by observing.

Solitary children (1 year)

Around the age of 12 months, children begin focusing on learning about and engaging in the world through their senses. Solitary play, which occurs when your child plays alone even when around other children, allows children to explore the world by touching, tasting and grabbing at toys, people and objects. Children discover relationships between their bodies and the environment and learn about cause and effect through solitary play.

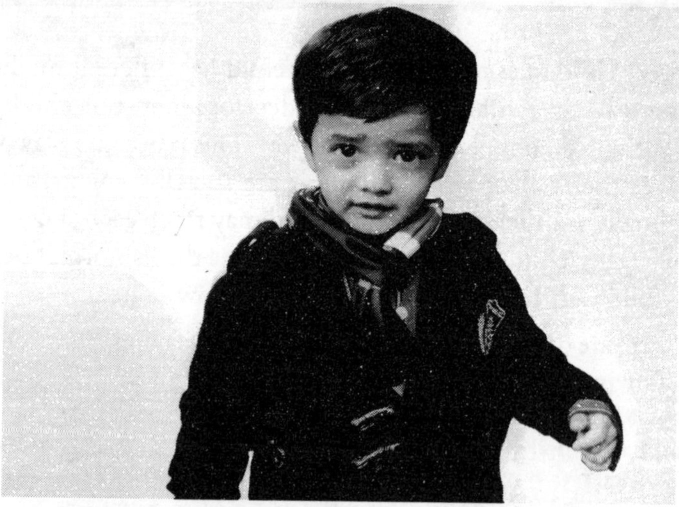

Parallel children (2 to 3 years/Toddlers)

Around the age of 2 to 3 years, children become more aware of the people in their world and move from solitary play to parallel play. Toddlers at this stage enjoy exploring their environment. As they play independently with toys, they start to see themselves as part of a social group. Children at this stage enjoy playing next to other children with the same game or activity, but they may not interact or play together. If we observe, two toddlers playing with building blocks at the same time, they typically don't talk about what they're doing or build a project together. Instead they work on building their own structure separate from each other.

Associative children (3 years and above)

Three-year-olds and above develop more interest in their peers and have more skills to interact successfully with other. At this point, most children will engage in associative play. While children at this stage may not work together at the same game, they like to watch and imitate those around them. Here, is an example: Two children at this stage may use the same clothes to play dress up and they may discuss what they're doing, but they don't play together to create a single game or imaginative narrative.

Cooperative children (6 years and above)

School age children typically have social skills that children younger than 3 years have not yet acquired and begin to form friendships as they enter the stage of co-operative play. At these stage children finally begin talking and working together during play. The two towers that toddlers build independently during parallel play become a single tower during cooperative play. The dress up acted out independently during associative play becomes a dramatic play story acted out together. Children at this stage of development learn to compromise and will seek help from adults to resolve conflicts. They are able to play elaborate games with rules and can enjoy organized sports or board games. They develop the feeling of togetherness, helpfulness and cooperate with each other.

CHAPTER 18 Children's Mother Development

Developmental Milestones

Age	Motor
1–1.5 months	When held upright, holds head erect and steady
1.5–2 months	When prone, lifts self by arms; rolls from side to back.
2.5–4.5 months	
3 months	Prone: head held up for prolonged periods. No grasp reflex
5 months	Holds head steady. Goes for objects and gets them. Objects taken to mouth
6 months	Transfers objects from one hand to the other. Pulls self up to sit and sits erect with supports. Rolls over prone to supine. PalmerHYPERLINK "http://en.wikipedia.org/wiki/Palmar_grasp" grasp of cube
9–10 months	Wiggles and crawls. Sits unsupported. Picks up objects with pincer grasp
1 year	Stands holding furniture. Stands alone for a second or two, then collapses with a bump
18 months	Can walk alone. Picks up toy without falling over. Gets up/down stairs holding onto rail. Begins to jump with both feet. Can build a tower of 3 or 4 cubes and throw a ball

2 years	Able to run. Walks up and down stairs 2 feet per step. Builds tower of 6 cubes
3 years	Goes up stairs 1-foot per step and downstairs 2 feet per step. Copies circle, imitates cross and draws man on request. Builds tower of 9 cubes
4 years	Goes down stairs one foot per step, skips on one foot. Imitates gate with cubes, copies a cross
5 years	Skips on both feet and hops. Draws a man and copies a triangle. Gives age
6 years	Copies a diamond. Knows right from left and number of fingers

Details of Specific Motor Development

A child's body movements and motor developments vary from age to age. Here, are the details of motor movements according to age. These movements are applied in general to all children. If there is a delay in any movement, parents should check.

1 to 4 Months' Motor development

- Upper body parts are more active: clasps hands above face, wave's arms about, reaches for objects.
- Turns head side to side when in a supine (face up) position; cannot hold head up and line with the body.
- Raises head and upper body on arms when in a prone position.
- Rooting and sucking reflexes are well developed.
- Swallowing reflex and tongue movements are immature; inability to move food to the back of the mouth.
- Grasp reflex.
- Movements are large and jerky.
- Grasps with entire hand; strength insufficient to hold items. Holds hands in an open or semi-open position.

5 to 8 Months' Motor development

- Blinking reflex is well established.
- Sucking reflex becomes voluntary.
- Reflexive behaviours are changing:
- Swallowing reflex appears and allows infant to move solid foods from front of mouth to the back for swallowing.
- When lowered suddenly, infant throws out arms as a protective measure.
- Picks up objects using finger and thumb.
- Reaches for objects with both arms simultaneously; later reaches with one hand or the other.
- Transfers objects from one hand to the other; grasps object using entire hand that is called palmerHYPERLINK "http://en.wikipedia.org/wiki/Palmar_grasp" grasp.
- Able to hold bottle.
- Handles, shakes, and pounds objects; puts everything in mouth.
- Sits alone without support, holding head erect, back straightened, and arms propped forward for support
- Pulls self into a crawling position by raising up on arms and drawing knees up beneath the body; rocks back and forth, but generally does not move forward.
- Can roll over from back or stomach position.
- May accidentally begin scooting backwards when placed on stomach; soon will begin to crawl forward.
- Lifts head when placed on back.
- Looks for fallen objects by 7 months.
- Does not understand "no" or "danger"

9 to 12 Months' Motor development

- Beginning to pull self to a standing position.
- Beginning to stand alone, leaning on furniture for support; moves around obstacles by side-stepping.
- Reaches with one hand leading to grasp an offered object or toy.
- Explores new objects by poking with one finger.
- Manipulates objects, transferring them from one hand to the other.
- Uses deliberate pincer grasp to pick up small objects, toys, and finger foods.
- Stacks objects; also places objects inside one another.
- Releases objects or toys by dropping or throwing; cannot intentionally put an object down.
- Has good balance when sitting; can shift positions without falling.
- Creeps on hands and knees; crawls up and down stairs.
- Walks with adult support, holding onto adult's hand; may begin to walk alone.
- Reaches for toys that are out of reach but visible.
- Drops thing intentionally and repeats and watches object.
- Imitates activities like playing drum.
- Watches people, objects, and activities in the immediate environment.
- Recognizes objects in reverse.
- Follows simple instructions.
- Responds to hearing tests (voice localization); however, loses interest quickly and, therefore, may be difficult to test formally.

- Begins to develop expressive language: The child actually responds to what is said to him.
- Enjoys eating different things of different tastes.
- Sometimes does not stop eating even when his tummy is full.

Learning to climb

Child learns to crawl up stairs

1 to 2 Years' Motor development

- Toddler crawls skilfully and quickly at the age of one year.
- Stands alone with feet spread apart, legs stiffened and arms extended for support and try to get support.
- Most children walk unassisted near the end of this period. Some children fall often, not always able to manoeuvre around obstacles, such as furniture or toys.
- Uses furniture to lower self to floor; collapses backwards into a sitting position or falls forward on hands and then sits.
- Attempts to run; has difficulty stopping and usually just drops to the floor.

- Crawls up stairs. Does not know how to step down. Sometimes goes down stairs in same position.
- Repeatedly picks up objects and throws them; direction becomes more deliberate.
- Enjoys pushing or pulling toys while walking.
- Carries toys from place to place.
- Sits in a small chair.
- Stacks two to six objects per day.
- Helps turn pages in book.
- Enjoys crayons and markers for scribbling; uses whole-arm movement.
- Helps feed self; enjoys holding spoon (often upside down) and drinking from a glass or cup.
- Not always accurate in getting utensils into mouth. Frequent spills should be expected.

Teeth Development

CHAPTER 19 Teeth Development of Child

Tooth eruption through the gum line in babies is called teething. The timing of tooth eruption differs from child to child. *For example*, one child may cut their first tooth when only a few months old, while another may not start teething until they are 12 months old or more.

Teething takes about eight days, which includes four days before and three days after the tooth comes through the gum. You may see a blue-grey bubble on the gum where the tooth is about to appear. This is called an eruption cyst and will usually go away without treatment. Generally, the average child has their full set of 20 primary teeth by the age of three years.

Primary teeth are also known as baby teeth, milk teeth or deciduous teeth. The development of the primary teeth begins while the baby is in the womb. At about five weeks' gestation, the first buds of primary teeth appear in the baby's jaws. At birth, the baby has a full set of 20 primary teeth (10 in the upper jaw, 10 in the lower jaw) hidden within the gums.

Types of Tooth

The names of the different types of tooth are:

- **Incisors:** The front teeth located in the upper and lower jaws. Each incisor has a thin cutting edge. The upper and lower incisors come together like a pair of scissors to cut the food.
- **Canines:** The pointy 'vampire' teeth on both sides of the incisors in the upper and lower jaws. They are used to tear food.

- **Premolars:** These have flat surfaces to crush food.
- **Molars:** These are larger than premolars, with broad, flat surfaces that grind food.

Order of Tooth Eruption

While the timing may vary, the order of tooth eruption is:

- The two front teeth (central incisors) in the lower jaw are usually the first to erupt. This occurs somewhere between the ages of four and 10 months.
- The two front teeth (central incisors) in the upper jaw erupt between the ages of six and 13 months.
- The lateral incisors, which are the teeth on each side of the central incisors, erupt in both the upper and lower jaws between the ages of eight and 16 months. The lower set tends to erupt before the upper set.
- The first set of upper and lower molars (flat-surfaced back teeth) erupt between the ages of 13 and 19 months.
- Canine or 'eye' teeth sit beside the lateral incisors and erupt in both the upper and lower jaws between the ages of 16 and 23 months.
- The second set of upper and lower molars erupts between the ages of 25 and 33 months.

Misconception about Teething and Illness

When babies are about six months old, the level of antibodies passed on from their mother starts to fall, which changes their immune systems. Alongwith the tendency to put things in their mouths, this makes them more prone to illnesses. Symptoms of common childhood illnesses such as changes in sleep and eating patterns, fussiness, rash, drooling, runny nose and diarrhoea are often mistakenly linked to teething.

If your child has these symptoms, make sure that they are not suffering from other possible causes such as bacterial, viral or middle ear infections.

Some tips for soothing sore gums include:

- **Massage:** Gently massage the sore gum with clean fingers or a soft, wet cloth
- **Chilled (not frozen) teething rings:** Pressure from a cold object can reduce inflammation and relieve discomfort from teething. Do not sterilise plastic teething rings in boiling water or dishwater, unless specified by the manufacturer. Be sure to check product information before buying teething rings. Avoid the ones that use a plastic softener
- **Unsweetened teething rusks or sugar-free teething biscuits:** These can be given to infants over six months who have started eating solids
- **Dry the drool:** The skin around the mouth, particularly the chin area, can become irritated. Gently wipe this away with a soft cloth throughout the day.

LOSS OF TEETH

Primary Teeth

Between the ages of about six and seven years, the primary teeth start to shed. The incisors are usually the first to go. Some children may worry about the loss of their first teeth, but the tooth fairy, with her cash reward for every shed tooth, usually helps to ease anxiety.

Eruption of permanent teeth

Permanent teeth are also known as adult teeth or secondary teeth. By about 21 years, the average person has 32 permanent teeth, including 16 in the upper jaw and 16 in the lower jaw. In some cases, however, the third molars – commonly called wisdom teeth – do not develop. Consequently, a set of 28 or 30 permanent teeth is considered normal too.

At about the age of six years, the first permanent teeth erupt. These four molars (two in each jaw) emerge behind the child's existing primary teeth. Other permanent teeth, such as the incisors and canines, erupt into the gaps in the gum left by shed primary teeth.

Like primary teeth, the timing for when the permanent teeth come through differs from one child to the next. Generally, the order of eruption and rough timeline for each type of permanent tooth is in the order of:

- **Central incisors:** between six and eight years
- **First molars:** between six and seven years
- **Lateral incisors:** between seven and eight years
- **Canine teeth:** between nine and 13 years
- **Premolars:** between nine and 13 years
- **Second molars:** between 11 and 13 years
- **Third molars (wisdom teeth):** between the ages of 17 and 21 years, if at all.

Important Things about Teeth

- Teething symptoms are common in children in the whole world and there is no need for medications.
- The average child has their full set of 20 primary teeth by the age of three years.
- Between the ages of about six and seven years, the primary teeth start to shed and the permanent teeth begin to come through.
- By the age of about 21 years, the average person has 32 permanent teeth–16 in the upper jaw and 16 in the lower jaw.
- A smile is the facial expression that most engages others. With the help of the teeth—which provide structural support for the face muscles—the mouth also forms a frown and other expressions that show on your face.

- The mouth also plays a key role in the digestive system, but it does much more than get digestion started. The mouth—especially the teeth, lips, and tongue —is essential for speech. With the lips and tongue, teeth help form words by controlling air flow out of the mouth. The tongue strikes the teeth as certain sounds are made.
- The hardest substances in the body, the teeth are also necessary for chewing. Teething is the process by which we tear, cut, and grind food in preparation for swallowing. Chewing allows enzymes and lubricants released in the mouth to further digest food.

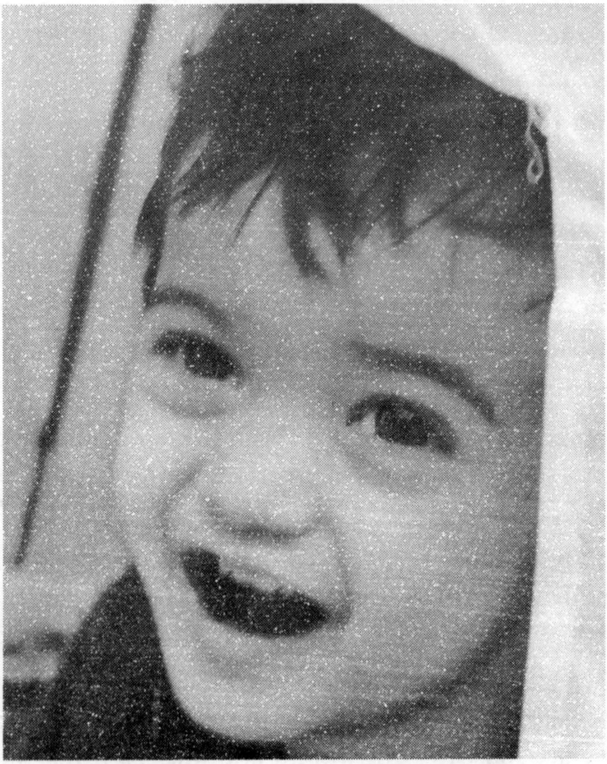

Teeth Make Face Attraction

CHAPTER 20 Intellectual and Cognitive Development in Early Childhood

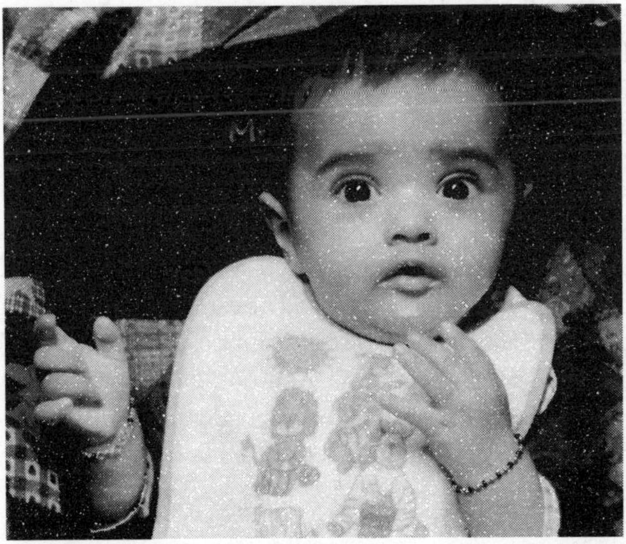

Early childhood, *i.e.*, from birth to five years, is a time of rapid intellectual development. According to the World Health Organization, it is the most important stage of development, and more than 200 million children in early childhood do not reach their full cognitive potential. An understanding of the cognitive milestones you can expect your child to reach, along with the knowledge of what he needs in order to thrive, can help you know if he is on the right track. If you are concerned about your child's intellectual development, be sure to talk to his doctor about his intellectual development.

Birth to 1 Year

It is very important period of life. Your child's cognitive development expands rapidly during the first year of his life. Responding to his needs and bonding with him in infancy helps to establish important neural connections. In just the first few months after birth, he learns to anticipate events and can distinguish the volume and pitch of different sounds. By 6 months of age, he is able to recognize faces and imitate facial expressions, and by 9 months, he can tell the difference between many objects and has some grasp of depth perception. At the age of 1-year, he has an understanding of object permanence and experiments regularly with objects to see how they work.

2 to 3 Years

During this period, your child expands intellectually through self-directed play and exploration. By 2 years of age, his language development is rapidly increasing and he can hold short conversations with adults. He is also able to spot similarities between objects and can properly use basic pronouns. At around 3 years old, he will also be able to group similar objects together, identify himself and engage in dramatic play in order to imitate adults. He can recite small rhymes.

4 to 5 Years

This period is known as preschool years. During this period your child is extremely curious and likely to ask a lot of questions about his environment. He also has a better sense of time and is able to identify parts of a whole. His attention span has increased from five to 15 minutes, and he is rapidly absorbing information by observing. Additionally, he is able to draw recognizable pictures and can tell you his name, age and town. He can recite 8 to 10 line rhymes easily.

How to Encourage Fast Development?

It is fact that your child will achieve a lot of his early childhood intellectual development through self-exploration and play. But there are steps you can take to encourage his development. According to the WHO, a lack of attachment to a consistent caregiver in the first months of life can negatively affect brain development. So make sure you are making an effort to bond, your child's diet is healthy and varied since a lack of nutrition can leave him unmotivated, tired, and unable to find the energy he needs to learn through play. Finally, provide him with plenty of space to explore and age-appropriate toys that he can play with.

CHAPTER 21 Details of Cognitive Development

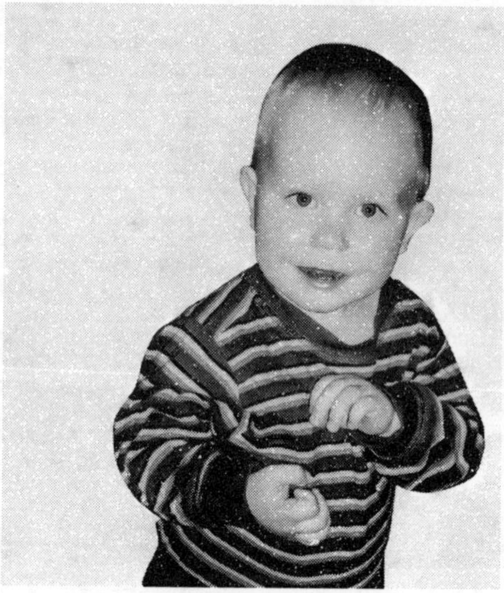

1 to 2 Years

- Enjoys looking at picture books.
- Names many everyday objects.
- Enjoys object-hiding activities.
- Early in this period, the child always searches in the same location for a hidden object (if the child has watched the hiding of an object). Later, the child will search in several locations.
- Manages three to four objects by setting an object aside (on lap or floor) when presented with a new toy.

- Passes toy to other hand when offered a second object (referred to as "crossing the midline" – an important neurological development).
- Puts toys in mouth less often.
- Shows or offers toy to another person to look at.
- Demonstrates understanding of functional relationships (objects that belong together). Shows increasing understanding of form discrimination: places geometric shapes in large form board or puzzle. Tries to join building blocks.
- Puts spoon in bowl and then uses spoon as if eating; places teacup on saucer and sips from cup; tries to make doll stand up.
- Places several small items (blocks, clothespins, cereal pieces) in a container or bottle and then dumps them out.
- Tries to make mechanical objects work after watching someone else do so.
- Responds with some facial movement, but cannot truly imitate facial expression.
- Most children with autism are diagnosed at this age.

2 Year Old

- Names familiar objects.
- Recognizes, expresses, and locates pain.

- Knows where familiar persons should be; notes their absence; finds a hidden object by looking in last hiding place first.
- Expresses more curiosity about the world.
- This is both a cognitive and linguistic advance that the child tells about objects and events not immediately present.
- Attends to self-selected activities for longer periods of time. Discovering cause and effect he knows that squeezing the cat makes her scratch.
- Eye–hand movements better co-ordinated; can put objects together, take them apart; fit large pegs into pegboard.
- Begins to use objects for purposes other than intended.
- Seems fascinated by, or engrossed in, figuring out situations: where the tennis ball rolled, where the dog went, what caused a particular noise.
- Does simple classification tasks based on single dimension. He can separate cars, utensils, building blocks etc.
- Expected to use magical thinking, such as believing a toy bear is a real bear.

The Differences in Gross Motor Development of Boys and Girls

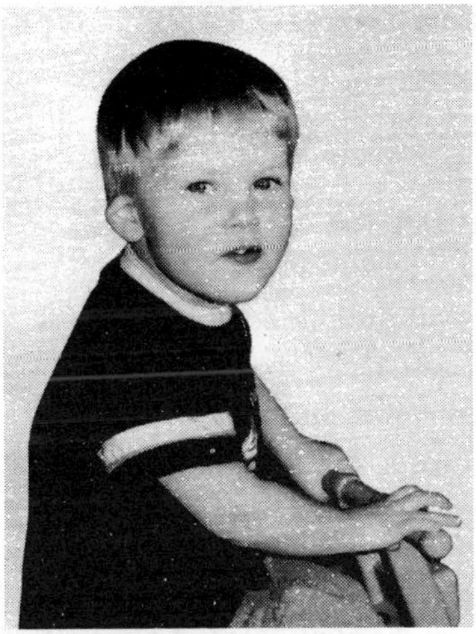

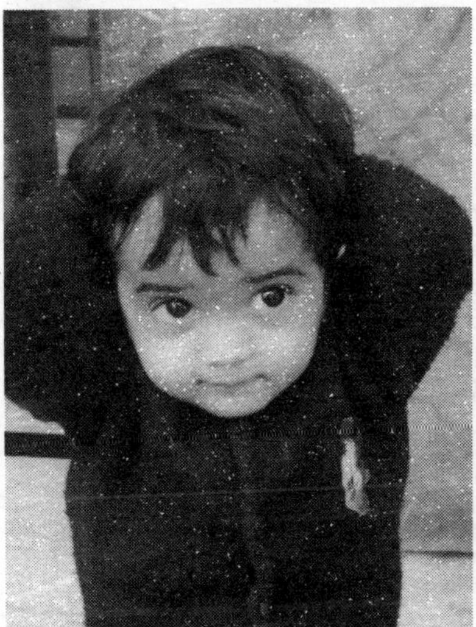

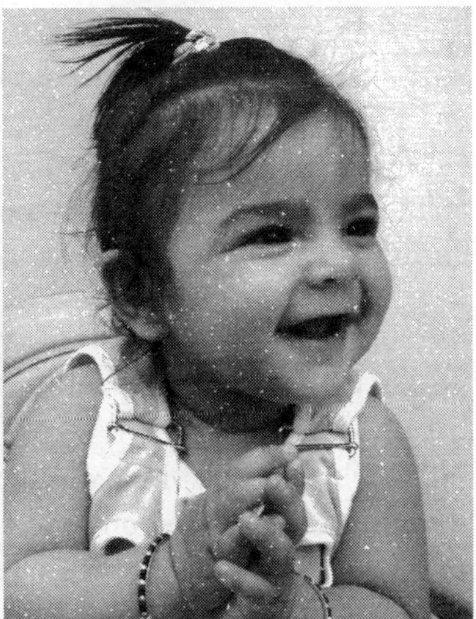

CHAPTER 22 The Differences in Gross Motor Development of Boys and Girls

Children in **early childhood** (from the age of 3 and above) experience rapid physical, mental and emotional changes and developments. Advancement of gross motor skills not only reflects muscular growth and dexterity, but brain development as well. Boys and girls typically mature at different rates, but gender differences also exist in how children use gross motor skills to play and interact with one another.

Gross Motor Development in Girls

The gender difference in gross motor skills in early childhood is slight. Girls typically develop these abilities at a slower rate. Girls are somewhat better than boys at skills that require balance and coordination, like hopping or skipping. Most parents direct the activities of girls differently than boys. Girls tend to develop fine motor skills, like those needed for drawing, faster than gross motor skills. As boys and girls move into middle childhood and adolescence, the difference in gross motor skills increases to a greater gap between genders.

Gross Motor Development in Boys

Between the ages of 3 and 6, a child's ability to run, jump, throw and catch improves dramatically, no matter the gender. However, according to researchers on child development, boys generally mature ahead of girls in skills that emphasize force and power. By the end of early childhood, boys can usually jump farther, run faster and throw a ball farther than girls. While some of the differences in development are genetic, Doctors points out that boys and girls are often routed into difference activities as a young child. For instance, fathers are more likely to play catching ball with their sons than with their daughters.

Gender Differences in Play and Behaviour

We can fine their behaviour differences by observing how children in early childhood play with one another. Researchers seek to understand the gender differences in physical, verbal and relational aggression. While a child's individual gross motor skill abilities do not directly affect how aggressive he or she will be. The difference between how boys and girls interact with the same gender provides insight into aggressive childhood behaviours. It is generally observed that boys show more physical and verbal aggressive behaviours than girls, often because they engage in more physical play.

Strengthening Gross Motor Skills of Children

To strengthen gross motor skills the preschoolers should participate daily in at least 60 minutes of aerobic and bone and muscle strengthening activities. All children, regardless of gender, can benefit from a home or school environment that purposefully provides opportunities to develop gross motor skills. When parents, family members and teachers intentionally encourage children to play physically, gross motor skills are enhanced. Having access to playgrounds with diverse types of equipment and time to explore and interact with other children outdoors increases opportunities for healthy physical development.

CHAPTER 23 Character Development of Children

Good character of a child shows his good parenting and care. Strong moral foundation is necessary to living a healthy and productive life in future. Base is always prepared in his/her childhood. The best way to increase the chances of raising children with positive character traits such as honesty, respect, courage, integrity and kindness is to teach him traits regularly and that you can implement over a length of time.

Helping children develop a strong moral character is an ongoing task, but it is one that is an essential part of raising children to become respectful adults who are both personally and professionally successful. Regularly incorporating crafts or hands-on educational activities into your child's play time can help him learn to develop positive character traits like gratitude, kindness and self-control.

What is good Character?

Be more concerned with your character than your reputation, because your character is what you really are, while your reputation is merely what others think you are. Character is what you are on the deepest level and what ultimately governs your actions. Character development teachings seek to shape an individual so that the foundation of that individual is positive. Positive character drives the individual to act in ways that are compassionate, honest, courageous, responsible and self-disciplined.

Identifying Traits of the Child

The traits of a character development should be listed that are vital to healthy and responsible living. That list can vary from one person to another. If a child is deficient in one or more of the listed traits, the parent can spend more time developing those traits and less time on the traits the child has mastered.

Teaching by Example

You can develop your Kids' character by using stories to help a child understand and nurture desirable traits. Children simply will not do what you tell them to do if you insist on doing the exact opposite. The stories and activities only provide the walls and roof of your character house — your living example provides the foundation your children build upon. That could make you self-conscious or it could inspire you to provide the best example your child could have.

Activities to Teach Character

Activity of Homemade "Thank You" Notes

This is a very easy and interesting activity for you to teach your child humble and thankful. Making thank you notes can teach young children about gratitude, creativity and thriftiness. Thank you notes can be sent for gifts your child has received or for special favours that someone has done. *For example*, a child could send a thank you note to Grandma that shows appreciation for the plate of chocolate chip cookies she sent over as an unexpected treat. Encourage your child to make homemade thank you notes using recycled materials such as old wrapping paper scraps or pretty pictures cut from junk mail you've received. Your child could also decorate his thank you notes with hand print art, such as a hand print heart made by overlapping two red hand prints.

Activity of Kindness Jar

To encourage kids to be kind, make an act of kindness jar from a clean glass jar and some strips of coloured construction paper. Write one example of an act of kindness on each slip of paper. Acts should be age-appropriate, but could include tasks such as helping a neighbour, washing the dishes after dinner without being asked or drawing a picture to send to a relative who lives far away or cleaning the table or bring the water for his father cleaning the room by removing toys etc. Every day or two let your child pick a strip from the jar and complete the activity. Put a coloured marble in a second jar each time your child finishes an act of kindness. When the second jar is full of marbles, plan a special family outing to celebrate. Sometimes you can give him his 'wish gift' after completing any one good task.

Character Trait by Puppet Shows

To teach your child about character traits in a fun and entertaining way, consider putting on a puppet show where he can demonstrate ways to show specific traits. You can either base your puppet shows on popular children's books or make up new stories together. For example, a puppet show about compassion and sensitivity could feature a dog who goes out of his way to become friends with a cat after the other dogs in the neighbourhood try to chase the cat away. A puppet show about responsibility could feature a boy who takes pride in taking care of his baby sister by making sure that she doesn't accidentally choke on one of his toys. There may be many other stories.

CHAPTER 24 Understanding Your Child

Understanding your child is one of the most important things that you should learn as a parent. It is very helpful in becoming effective in guiding and nurturing your child as he grows and matures. You need to bear in mind that your child has a unique personality trait that remains consistent throughout life.

One of the ways you can understand your child is by observing them as he sleeps, eats, or plays. Look for the consistent traits. Which activities does he like best? Is adjusting to changes easy for him or does he need time to become familiar with these things? These things are the normal characteristics of a child and your child may not be an exception.

You should devote time as much as possible to talk to your children as this is crucial to gaining information and understanding. In the case of young child, he requires less verbal language and more facial expression and body language in order to understand his thoughts and feelings.

Asking question to the child will allow him to share his feeling with you. Here is an example, rather than asking him what he did in school, ask him what he built with his blocks today.

Another way of understanding your child is by taking a look at his environment in order to learn about a certain behaviour that you have observed. Relatives, child care maids, friends, teachers, the home setting and other aspects of the environment can play a crucial role in the behaviour of your child. *For example*, if your child is showing aggressiveness towards other children at school, you may want to find out all the possible sources of his aggressive behaviour.

The environment at home is another possible source for such behaviour. Have there been conflicts and arguments at home lately that was seen by your child? What about in the community? These are some angles that you should consider when trying to find the reason behind your child's aggressive behaviour.

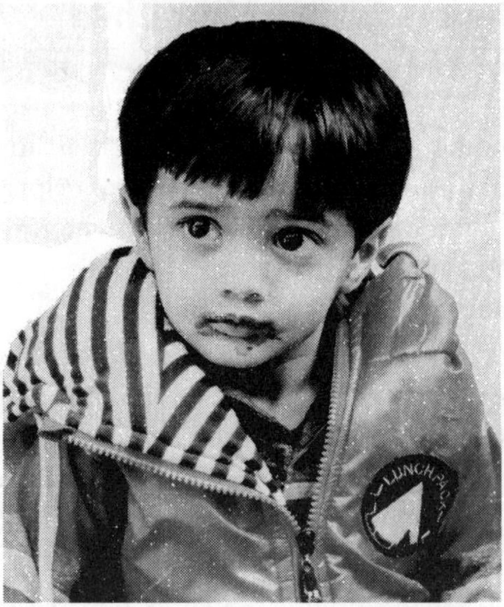

Besides this you can learn about your child by observing other children belonging to the similar age group. Bear in mind that you went through the same stages as a child so more or less the behaviour of children in that same stage would be similar. However, the speed of development through each stage is a personal thing.

If you understand your child's development, you will be able to provide him with opportunities as well as toys that can boost his development and prepare him for the next phase of his growth. At the same time, you as a parent would be able to set expectations and limits that are acceptable to your child.

Understanding your child is one effective way of becoming successful in the art of parenting.

Speech and Language Development

CHAPTER 25 Speech and Language Development

In the first 3 years of life, the brain continues developing and maturing. It is the most intensive period for acquiring speech and language skills. These skills develop best in a world that is rich with sounds, sights and consistent exposure to the speech and language of others.

Infants and young children the brain is best able to absorb language. If these critical periods are allowed to pass without exposure to language, it will be more difficult to learn.

Difference in voice, speech and language

Voice, speech, and language are the tools we use to communicate with each other.

Voice is the sound we make as air from our lungs is pushed between vocal folds in our larynx, causing them to vibrate.

Speech is talking, which is one way to express language. It involves the precisely co-ordinated muscle actions of the tongue, lips, jaw and vocal tract to produce the recognizable sounds that make up language.

Language is a set of shared rules that allow people to express their ideas in a meaningful way. Language may be expressed verbally or by writing, signing, or making other gestures, such as eye blinking or mouth movements.

Difference between a speech disorder and a language disorder

Children who have trouble understanding what others say (receptive language) or difficulty sharing their thoughts (expressive language) may have a language disorder. Specific Language Impairment (SLI) is a language disorder that delays the mastery of language skills. Some children with SLI may not begin to talk until their third or fourth year.

Children who have trouble producing speech sounds correctly or who hesitate or stutter when talking may have a speech disorder. Apraxia of speech is a speech disorder that makes it difficult to put sounds and syllables together in the correct order to form words.

Some children feel shy while talking and speaking

CHAPTER 26 Milestones of Language, Speech and Communication upto 8 Years

Birth to 3 Months

- Reacts to loud sounds.
- Calms down or smiles when spoken to.
- Recognizes your voice and calms down if crying.
- Coos and makes pleasure sounds.
- When feeding, starts or stops sucking in response to sound.
- Smiles when he or she sees you.
- Has a special way of crying for different needs.

4 to 6 Months

- Follows sounds with his or her eyes.
- Notices toys that make sounds.
- Responds to changes in the tone of your voice.
- Pays attention to music.
- Babbles in a speech-like way and uses many different sounds, including sounds that begin with p, b, and m.
- Laughs.
- Babbles when excited or unhappy.
- Makes gurgling sounds when alone or playing with you.

7 Months to 1 Year

- Listens when spoken to.
- Turns and looks in the direction of sounds.

- Understands words for common items such as "cup," "shoe," or "juice".
- Babbles using long and short groups of sounds ("tata, upup, bibibi").
- Babbles to get and keep attention.
- Responds to requests ("Come here" or "Want more?").
- Communicates using gestures such as waving or holding up arms.
- Has one or two words ("Hi," "dog," "Dada," or "Mama") by first birthday.
- Imitates different speech sounds.

1 to 2 Years

- Knows a few parts of the body and can point to them when asked.
- Enjoys simple stories, songs, and rhymes.
- Points to pictures, when named, in books.
- Acquires new words on a regular basis.
- Follows simple commands ("Roll the ball") and understands simple questions ("Where's your shoe?")
- Uses some one- or two-word questions ("Where, what" or "Go bye-bye?")
- Puts two words together ("More cookie" or "No juice")
- Uses many different consonant sounds at the beginning of words .

Receptive language	Expressive language
• Learn that words he hears. • Usually recognize the names of meaning family members and familiar objects. • Understand simple statements such as "all gone" and "give me." • Between 1 and 2 years, understand simple requests such as "give daddy the ball." • By 18 months, know the names of people, body parts, and objects.	• Use gestures, such as pointing. • Babble less than babies do. • Often make one- or two-syllable sounds that stand for items they want, such as "baba" for "bottle" and point to things they want. • Between 12 months and 18 months of age, may use their own language, sometimes called jargon, that is a mix of made-up words and understandable words. • Between 1 and 2 years, usually can say between 20 and 50 words that are intelligible to family members.

2 to 3 Years

- Uses two- or three-word phrases to talk about and ask for things.
- Has a word for almost everything.
- Uses k, g, f, t, d and n sounds.
- Names objects to ask for them or to direct attention to them.
- Speaks in a way that is understood by family members and friends.

Receptive Language	Expressive Language
• Know the name of at least seven body parts. • Increase their understanding of object names. • Follow simple requests (such as "put the book on the table"). • When asked, point to a picture of something named (such as "Where is the cow?" or "Show me the airplane.")	• Continue to learn and use gestures. • Sometimes talk a lot, although some are quiet. • If quiet, develop a communication system using gestures and facial expressions; are likely to develop normal language skills. • Usually can name some body parts (such as arms and legs), favourite toys and familiar objects (such as cats and dogs). • Use pronouns like "me" and "you," but they often get them mixed up. • Can make phrases, such as "no bottle" or "want cookie." • By age 3, usually can say between 150 to 200 words. Strangers can understand them about 75% of the time.

3 to 4 Years

- Hears the television or radio at the same sound level as other family members.
- Hears you when you call from another room.
- Answers simple "Who?" "What?" "Where?" and "Why?" questions.
- Uses sentences with four or more words.

- Talks about activities at day-care, preschool, or friends' homes.
- Speaks easily without having to repeat syllables or words.

4 to 5 Years

- Can use many descriptive words spontaneously-both adjectives and adverbs.
- Can count to ten.
- Speech should be completely intelligible, in spite of articulation problems.
- Tomorrow, yesterday, today.
- Should be able to define common objects in terms of use (hat, shoe, chair).
- Should be able to follow three commands given without interruptions.
- Has a number concept of 4 or more.
- Knows common opposites: big-little, hard-soft, heave-light, etc.
- Should know his age.
- Speech on the whole should be grammatically correct
- Should be using fairly long sentences and should use some compound and some complex sentences.
- Should be able to repeat sentences as long as nine words.
- Should have simple time concepts: morning, afternoon, night, day, later, after, while.

5 to 6 Years

- Should understand differences between objects and happenings.
- Should be able to tell one a rather connected story about a picture, seeing relationships.
- In addition to the above consonants these should be mastered: f, v, sh, zh, th,1.

- Speech should be completely intelligible and socially useful.
- He should have concepts of 7.

6 to 7 Years

- Should be able to tell time to quarter hour.
- Should have mastered the consonants s-z, r, voiceless th, ch, wh, and the soft g as in George.
- Understands such terms as: alike, different, beginning, end, etc.
- Should handle opposite analogies easily: girl-boy, man-woman, flies-swims, blunt-sharp short-long, sweet-sour, etc.
- Should be able to do simple reading and to write or print many words.

7 to 8 Years

- Complex and compound sentences should be used easily.
- Should be few lapses in grammatical constrictions-tense, pronouns, plurals.
- Has well developed time and number concepts.
- Social amenities should be present in his speech in appropriate situations.
- Follows fairly complex directions with little repetition.
- Should be reading with considerable ease and now writing simple compositions.
- All speech sounds, including consonant blends should be established.
- Can relate rather involved accounts of events, many of which occurred at some time in the past.
- Control of rate, pitch, and volume are generally well and appropriately established.
- Can carry on conversation at rather adult level.

CHAPTER 27 Speech and Language Disorders

If you feel that your child is slow in learning language or delayed the milestones, talk to your child's doctor. Your doctor may refer you to a speech-language pathologist, who is a health professional trained to evaluate and treat people with speech or language disorders. The speech-language pathologist will talk to you about your child's communication and general development. The pathologist will also use special spoken tests to evaluate your child. A hearing test is often included in the evaluation because a hearing problem can affect speech and language development. Depending on the result of the evaluation, the speech-language pathologist may suggest activities you can do at home to stimulate your child's development. They might also recommend group or individual therapy or suggest further evaluation by an audiologist. Who will measure hearing loss or a psychologist will check the psychological development of infants and children.

Most 1-year-olds begin to understand the meanings of words. Their receptive language grows from understanding names of people and objects, to being able to follow simple requests sometime between ages 1 and 2. Expressive language advances from primarily using gestures and babbling at age 1, to using words, simple phrases, and some early sentence structures between ages 2 and 3. Your child is 2 years old and still isn't talking. He/she says a few words, but compared with his/her peers you think he's way behind. You remember that his sister could put whole sentences together at the same age. Hoping he will catch up, you postpone seeking professional advice. Some kids are early walkers and some are early talkers, you tell yourself. Nothing to worry about this scenario is common among parents of kids who are slow to speak. Unless they observe other areas of "slowness" during early development, parents hesitate to seek advice. Some may excuse the lack of talking by reassuring themselves that "he'll outgrow it" or "she's just more interested in physical things." But if you are not sure about slow development, seek the help of specialist or a doctor.

WARNING OF YOUR CHILD'S SPEECH PROBLEMS

If you're concerned about your child's speech and language development, there are some things to watch for. An infant who isn't responding to sound or who isn't vocalizing is a matter of concern. At the age of 1 to 2 years, you should be concerned with your child's speech. Look,

If the child:

- isn't using gestures, such as pointing or waving bye-bye, by 12 months
- prefers gestures over vocalizations to communicate at 18 months
- has trouble imitating sounds by 18 months
- has difficulty understanding simple verbal requests

Consult the doctor, if a child is over 2 years old:

- can only imitate speech or actions and doesn't produce words or phrases spontaneously
- can't follow simple directions
- says only certain sounds or words repeatedly and can't use oral language to communicate more than his or her immediate needs
- has an unusual tone of voice (such as raspy or nasal sounding)
- is more difficult to understand than expected for his or her age. Parents and regular parents should understand about half

of a child's speech at 2 years and about three quarters at 3 years. By 4 years old, a child should be mostly understood, even by people who don't know the child.

CAUSES OF DELAYED SPEECH AND LANGUAGE

Many things can cause delays in speech and language development of a child. Speech delays in a normally developing child can sometimes be caused by oral impairments, like problems with the tongue or palate (the roof of the mouth). A short frenulum (the fold beneath the tongue) can limit tongue movement for speech production.

Many children with speech delays have oral-motor problems, meaning there's inefficient communication in the areas of the brain responsible for speech production. The child encounters difficulty using and co-ordinating the lips, tongue and jaw to produce speech sounds. Speech may be the only problem or may be accompanied by other oral-motor problems such as feeding difficulties. A speech delay may also be a part of a more important developmental delay.

Ear infections, especially chronic infections, can affect hearing ability. Simple ear infections that have been adequately treated, though, should have no effect on speech. And, as long as there is normal hearing in at least one ear, speech and language will develop normally.

Hearing problems are also commonly related to delayed speech, which is why a child's hearing should be tested by an audiologist whenever there's a speech concern. A child who has trouble hearing may have trouble articulating as well as understanding, imitating, and using language.

CHAPTER 28 Milestones of Vision and Hearing Development

DEVELOPMENTAL MILESTONES

Age	Vision and Hearing
1-1.5 months	
1.5-2 months	Focuses on objects as well as adults
2.5-4.5 months	Hand regard: following the hand with the eyes.[3] Color vision adult-like.
3 months	Follows dangling toy from side to side. Turns head round to sound. Follows adults' gaze (joint attention). Sensitivity to binocular cues emerges.
5 months	
6 months	Localises sound 45 cm lateral to either ear. Visual acuity adult-like (20/20). Sensitivity to pictorial depth cues (those used by artists to indicate depth) emerges.
9-10 months	Looks for toys dropped
1 year	Drops toys and watches where they go

Social and emotional development

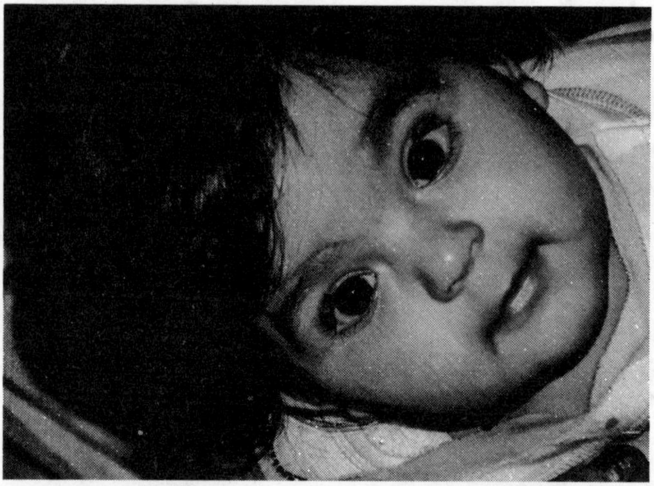

CHAPTER 29 Social and Emotional Development

Child's social and emotional development is as important as physical and other development. Social-emotional development includes the child's experience, expression and management of emotions and the ability to establish positive and rewarding relationships with others. It encompasses both intra- and interpersonal processes.

The features of emotional development include the ability to identify and understand one's own feelings, to accurately read and comprehend emotional states in others, to manage strong emotions and their expression in a constructive manner, to regulate one's own behaviour, to develop empathy for others and to establish and maintain relationships.

Emotional development begins since childhood

Infants experience, express and perceive emotions before they fully understand them. In learning to recognize, label, manage and communicate their emotions and to perceive and attempt to understand the emotions of others, children build skills that connect them with family, peers, teachers, and the community. These growing capacities help young children to become competent in negotiating increasingly complex social interactions, to participate effectively in relationships and group activities and to reap the benefits of social support crucial to healthy human development and functioning.

Healthy social-emotional development for infants and toddlers unfolds in an interpersonal context, namely that of positive ongoing relationships with familiar adults. Young children are particularly attuned to social and emotional stimulation. Even newborns appear to attend more to stimuli that resemble faces. They also prefer their mothers' voices to the voices of other women.

Responsive care giving supports infants in beginning to regulate their emotions and to develop a sense of predictability, safety, and responsiveness in their social environments. Early relationships are very important to developing infants. Nurturing, stable and consistent relationships are the key to healthy growth, development and learning. In other words, high-quality relationships increase the likelihood of positive outcomes for young children. Experiences with family members and teachers provide an opportunity for young children to learn about social relationships and emotions.

Emotions and social behaviours affect the young child's ability to persist in goal-oriented activity, to seek help when it is needed, and to participate in and benefit from relationships.

Young children who exhibit healthy social, emotional, and behavioural adjustment are more likely to have good academic performance in elementary school.

Milestones of Emotional and Social Development

Birth to1 month	Feedings: 5-8 per day, Sleep: 20 hrs per day
2 months to3 months	Sensory Capacities: Colour perception, visual exploration, oral exploration. Sounds: Cries, coos, grunts Motor Ability: control of eye muscles, lifts head when on stomach. Delight
4 months to 6 months	Sensory Capacities: Localizes sounds: babbling makes most vowels and about half of the consonants.

7 months to 9 months	Motor Ability: Control of trunk and hands, sits without support, crawls about.
10 months to 12 months	Motor Ability: Control of legs and feet, stands, creeps, apposition of thumb and fore-finger.
1 years to 1 ½ years	Motor Ability: Creeps up stairs, walks (10-20 min), makes lines on paper with crayon. Dependent Behaviour
1 ½ years to 2 years	Motor Ability: Runs, kicks a ball, builds 6 cube tower (2yrs) Capable of bowel and bladder control. Language: vocabulary of more than 200 words Sleep: 12 hours at night, 1-2 hr nap
2 years to 3 years	Motor Ability: Jumps off a step, rides a tricycle, uses crayons, builds a 9-10 cube tower. Language: Starts to use short sentences controls and explores world with language, stuttering may appear briefly. Fear of separation
3 years to 4 years	Motor Ability: Stands on one leg, jumps up and down, draws a circle and a cross (4 yrs)
4 years to 5 years	Motor ability: Mature motor control, skips, broad jumps, dresses himself, copies a square and a triangle. Language: talks clearly, uses adult speech sounds, has mastered basic grammar, relates a story, knows over 2,000 words(5 yrs)

CHAPTER 30 Specific Detail of all Developments of 2 Year Old and Above

PHYSICAL DEVELOPMENT

Two-Year-Old

- Brain reaches about 80 percent of its adult size.
- Body temperature continues to fluctuate with activity, emotional state and environment.
- Respirations are slow and regular.
- 16 baby teeth almost finished growing out
- Posture is more erect; abdomen still large and protruding, back swayed, because abdominal muscles are not yet fully developed.

Three-Year-Old

- Legs grow faster than arms,
- Growth is steady though slower than in first two years.
- Circumference of head and chest is equal; head size is in better proportion to the body.
- Adult height can be predicted from measurements of height at three years of age; males are approximately 53% of their adult height and females, 57%.
- Slightly knock-kneed.
- "Baby fat" disappears as neck appears.
- Posture is more erect; abdomen no longer protrudes.
- Can jump from low step.
- Can stand up and walk around on tiptoes.
- "baby" teeth stage over.
- Needs to consume approximately 1,500 calories daily.

Four-Year-Old

- Hearing acuity can be assessed by child's correct usage of sounds and language, and also by the child's appropriate responses to questions and instructions.
- Head circumference is usually not measured after age three.
- Requires approximately 1,700 calories daily.

Five-Year-Old

- May begin to lose "baby" (deciduous) teeth.
- Head size is approximately that of an adult's.
- Body is adult-like in proportion.
- Visual tracking and binocular vision are well developed.
- Requires approximately daily.

Six-Year-Old

- Heart rate and respiratory rates are close to adults.
- Body may appear lanky as through period of rapid growth.
- Weight gains reflect significant increases in muscle mass.
- Baby teeth beginning to be replaced by permanent ones, starting with the two lower front teeth.
- 20/20 eyesight; if below 20/40 should see a professional.
- The most common vision problem during middle childhood is myopia, or nearsightedness. (Berk, 2007).
- Uses 6,700 J to 7,100 J (1,600 to 1,700 calories) a day.

MOTOR DEVELOPMENT

Two-Year-Old

- Balances on one foot (for a few moments), jumps up and down, but may fall.
- Can climb stairs unassisted, but cannot climb with alternating feet.
- Can walk around obstacles and walk more erect.
- Squats for long periods while playing.
- Throws large ball underhand without losing balance. Holds

small cup or tumbler in one hand. Unbuttons large buttons; unzips large zippers.

- Opens doors by turning doorknobs.
- Grasps large crayon with fist; scribbles.
- Stacks four to six objects on top of one another.
- Uses feet to propel wheeled riding toys.
- Climbs up on chair, turns, and sits down.
- Often achieves toilet training during this year (depending on child's physical and neurological development) although accidents should still be expected; the child will indicate readiness for toilet training.

Three-Year-Old

- Can kick big ball-shaped objects.
- Needs minimal assistance eating.
- Jumps on the spot.
- Can momentarily balance on one foot.
- Walks up and down stairs unassisted, using alternating feet; may jump from bottom step, landing on both feet.
- Throws a ball overhand; aim and distance are limited.
- Catches a large bounced ball with both arms extended.
- Pedals a small tricycle.
- Enjoys swinging on a swing.
- Holds crayon or marker between first two fingers and thumb (tripod grasp), not in a fist as earlier.
- Builds a tower of eight or more blocks. Enjoys building with blocks.
- Can turn pages of a book one at a time.
- Shows improved control of crayons or markers; uses vertical, horizontal and circular strokes.
- Enjoys playing with clay; pounds, rolls, and squeezes it.
- May begin to show hand dominance.

- Carries a container of liquid, such as a cup of milk or bowl of water, without much spilling; pours liquid from pitcher into another container.
- Manipulates large buttons and zippers on clothing.
- Washes and dries hands; brushes own teeth, but not thoroughly.
- Usually achieves complete bladder control during this time.

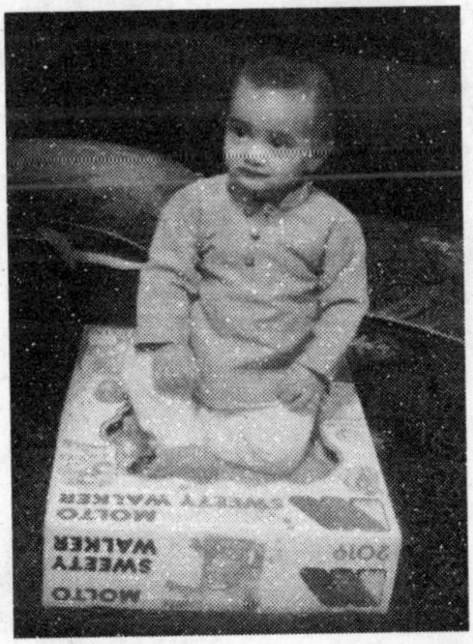

Four-Year-Old

- Hops on one foot.
- Climbs ladders, trees, playground equipment.
- Pedals and steers a wheeled toy with confidence; turns corners, avoids obstacles and oncoming "traffic."
- Walks a straight line (tape or chalk line on the floor).
- Runs, starts, stops, and moves around obstacles with ease.
- Jumps over objects 5 to 6 inch high; lands with both feet together.
- Forms shapes and objects out of clay: Cookies, snakes, simple animals.
- Builds a tower with ten or more blocks.
- Throws a ball overhand; distance and aim improving.

- Reproduces some shapes and letters.
- Can run in a circle.
- Threads small wooden beads on a string.
- Holds a crayon or marker using a tripod grasp.
- Paints and draws with purpose; may have an idea in mind, but often has problems implementing it so calls the creation something else.

Five-Year-Old

- Walks unassisted up and down stairs, alternating feet.
- May learn to turn somersaults.
- Walks backwards, toe to heel.
- Can touch toes without flexing knees.
- Walks a balance beam.
- Learns to skip using alternative feet.
- Catches a ball thrown from 1 m away.
- Jumps or hops forward ten times in a row without falling.
- Balances on either foot with good control for ten seconds.
- Builds three-dimensional structures with small cubes by copying from a picture or model.

- Rides a tricycle or wheeled toy with speed and skillful steering; some children learning to ride bicycles, usually with training wheels.
- Often has an imaginary friend.
- Hand dominance is fairly well established.
- Cuts on the line with scissors (not perfectly).
- Reproduces many shapes and letters: square, triangle, A, I, O, U, C, H, L, T.
- Demonstrates fair control of pencil or marker; may begin to color within the lines.

Six-Year-Old

- Has trouble staying still.
- Enjoys vigorous running, jumping, climbing and throwing etc.
- Span of attention increases; works at tasks for longer periods of time, though
- Can concentrate effort but not always consistently.
- Recognizes seasons and major activities done in the times.
- Understands time (today, tomorrow, yesterday) and simple motion (things go faster than others).
- Has fun with problem solving and sorting activities like stacking, puzzles and mazes

- Enjoys the challenge of puzzles, counting and sorting activities, paper-and-pencil mazes and games that involve matching letters and words with pictures.
- Recognizes some words by sight; attempts to sound out words
- In some cases the child may be reading well.
- Enjoys making things.
- Reverses or confuse certain letters: b/d, p/g, g/q, t/f.
- Folds and cuts paper into simple shapes.
- Can tie Laces, string of shoes.
- Able to trace objects.
- Gains greater control over large and fine motor skills; movements are more precise and deliberate, though some clumsiness persists.
- Functioning which facilitates learning to ride a bicycle, swim, swing a bat, or kick a ball.

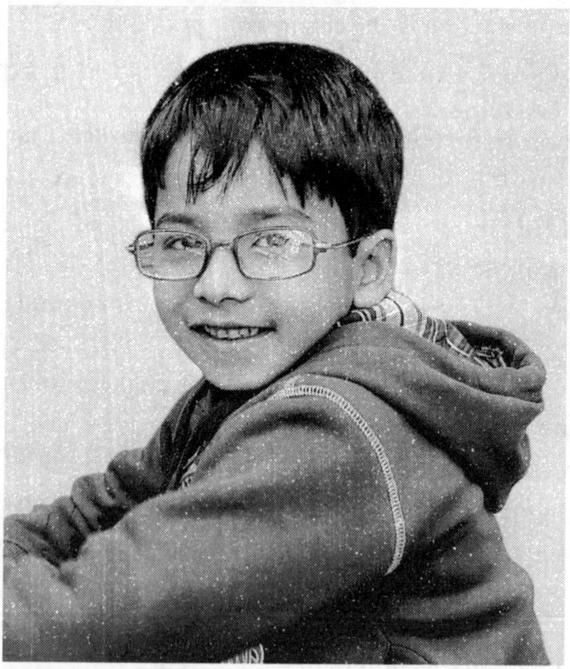

COGNITIVE DEVELOPMENT

Two Year Old

- Names familiar objects.
- Recognizes, expresses and locates pain.
- Knows where familiar persons should be; notes their absence; finds a hidden object by looking in last hiding place first.
- Expresses more curiosity about the world.
- This is both a cognitive and linguistic advance. Tells about objects and events not immediately present that the child.
- Attends to self-selected activities for longer periods of time. Discovering cause and effect he knows that squeezing the cat makes her scratch.
- Eye–hand movements better coordinated; can put objects together, take them apart; fit large pegs into pegboard.
- Begins to use objects for purposes other than intended.
- Seems fascinated by, or engrossed in, figuring out situations: where the tennis ball rolled, where the dog went, what caused a particular noise.
- Does simple classification tasks based on single dimension. He can separate cars, utensils, building blocks etc.
- Expected to use "magical thinking", such as believing a toy bear is a real bear.

Three-Year-Old

- Makes relevant comments during stories, especially those that relate to home and family events.
- Likes to look at books and may pretend to "read" to others or explain pictures.
- Enjoys stories with riddles, guessing, and "suspense."
- Listens attentively to age-appropriate stories.
- Speech is understandable most of the time.
- Produces expanded noun phrases: "big, brown dog."
- Indicates negatives by inserting "no" or "not" before a simple

noun or verb phrase: "Not baby."

- Answers "What are you doing?", "What is this?", and "Where?" questions dealing with familiar objects and events.
- Produces verbs with "ing" endings; uses "-s" to indicate more than one; often puts "-s" on already pluralized forms: geeses, mices.

Four-Year-Old

- Names eighteen to twenty uppercase letters. Writes several letters and sometimes his name.
- A few children are beginning to read simple books, such as alphabet books with only a few words per page and many pictures.
- Can recognize that certain words sound similar.
- Delights in wordplay, creating silly Language.
- Likes stories about how things grow and how things operate.
- Understands the concepts of "tallest," "biggest," "same," and "more"; selects the picture that has the "most houses" or the "biggest dogs."
- Follows two to three step directions given individually or in a group
- May put the "ed" on the end of words such as "I goed outside and I played."
- Counts 1 to 7 objects out loud, but not always in order.
- Counts to 20 or more.
- Understands the sequence of daily events: "When we get up in the morning, we get dressed, have breakfast, brush our teeth, and go to school."
- When looking at pictures can recognize and identify missing puzzle parts (of person, car, animal, bird etc).
- Very good storyteller.

Five-Year-Old

- Builds steps with set of small blocks.
- Understands concept of same shape, same size.

- Sorts objects on the basis of two dimensions, such as colour and form.
- Forms rectangle from two triangular cuts.
- Understands the concepts of smallest and shortest; places objects in order from shortest to tallest, smallest to largest.
- Sorts a variety of objects so that all things in the group have a single common feature.
- Identifies objects with specified serial position: first, second, last.
- Understands the terms dark, light and early: "I got up early, before anyone else. It was still dark."
- Understands the concepts of less than: "Which bowl has less water?"
- Recognizes numerals from 1 to 10.
- Rote counts to 20 and above; many children count to 100.
- Some children can tell time on the hour: Five o'clock, two o'clock.
- Relates clock time to daily schedule: "Time to turn on TV when the little hand points to 5."
- Knows what a calendar is for.
- Eager to learn new things.
- Asks innumerable questions: Why? What? Where? When? How?
- Recognizes and identifies coins; beginning to count and save money.
- Understands the concept of half; can say how many pieces an object has when it's been cut in half.

Six-Year-Old

- Tremendous learning growth.
- Tackles more difficult material.
- They will begin to read and may even delve into chapter books.
- Will learn basic math skills.
- Will learn subject such as art, science, and history.

SOCIAL AND EMOTIONAL DEVELOPMENT

Two Year Old

- Shows signs of empathy and caring.
- Sometimes appears to be overly affectionate in offering hugs and kisses to children.
- Comforts another child if hurt or frightened.
- Continues to use physical aggression if frustrated or angry (for some children, this is more exaggerated than for others); Physical aggression usually lessens as verbal skills improve.
- Impatient; finds it difficult to wait or take turns.
- Temper tantrums likely to peak during this year; extremely difficult to reason with during a tantrum.
- Enjoys "helping" with household chores; imitates everyday activities: may try to toilet train a stuffed animal, feed a doll.
- Making choices is difficult; wants it both ways.
- Offers toys to other children, but is usually possessive of playthings; still tends to hoard toys.
- Ritualistic; wants everything "just so"; routines carried out exactly as before; belongings placed "where they belong."
- Watches and imitates the play of other children, but seldom interacts directly; plays near others, often choosing similar toys and activities, solitary play is often simple and repetitive.
- "Bossy" with parents and elders; orders them around, makes demands, expects immediate compliance from adults.
- Often defiant; shouting "no" becomes automatic.

Three Year Old

- Enjoy Parallel play.
- Enjoys being by others.
- Knows if he is a boy or girl.
- Enjoys brief group activities requiring no skill.
- Takes turns.

- Likes to "help" in small ways–responds to verbal guidance.
- Seems sure of himself.
- Needs controlled freedom.
- May be defiant.
- Out-of bounds behaviour.
- Seems to be testing himself out.
- Often negative.

Four Year Old

- Moods change rapidly and unpredictably; laughing one minute, crying the next; may throw tantrum over minor frustrations for example far a block structure that will not balance.
- Outgoing; friendly; over enthusiastic at times.
- Imaginary playmates or companions are common; holds conversations and shares strong emotions with this invisible friend.
- Cooperates with others; participates in group activities.
- Shows pride in accomplishments; seeks frequent adult approval.
- Often appears selfish; not always able to take turns or to understand taking turns under some conditions; tattles on other children.
- Boasts, exaggerates, and "bends" the truth with made-up stories or claims of boldness; tests the limits with "bathroom" talk.
- Establishes close relationships with playmates; beginning to have "best" friends.
- Name-calling and taunting are often used as ways of excluding other children.
- Relies most of the time on verbal rather than Physical aggression; may yell angrily rather than hit to make a point; threatens: "You can't come to my birthday party"

- Enjoys role-playing and make-believe activities.
- Insists on trying to do things independently, but may get so frustrated as to verge on tantrums when problems arise: paint that drips, paper airplane that will not fold right.

Five Year Old

- Plays cooperatively, is generous, takes turns, shares toys.
- Participates in group play and shared activities with other children; suggests imaginative and elaborate play ideas.
- Enjoys and often has one or two focus friendships.
- Shows affection and caring towards others especially those "below" them or in pain.
- Often has an imaginary friend.
- Boasts about accomplishments.
- Likes entertaining people and making them laugh.
- Has better self-control over swings of emotions.
- Needs comfort and reassurance from adults but is less open to comfort.

Six Years Old

- Has mood swings towards primary caregiver or parents depending on the day.
- Friendship with parent is less depended on but still needs closeness and nurturing.
- Uses language rather than tantrums or physical aggression to express displeasure: "That's mine! Give it back, you dumbo."
- Anxious to please; needs and seeks adult approval, reassurance, and praise; may complain excessively about minor hurts to gain more attention.
- Talks self through steps required in simple problem-solving situations though the "logic" may be unclear to adults.
- Often can't view the world from another's point of view.

- May be increasingly fearful of the unknown like things in the dark, noises, and animals.
- Understands when he or she has been thought to be "bad"; values are based on others' enforced values.
- Can't handle things not going their own way.
- Self-perceived failure can make the child easily disappointed and frustrated.
- Does not understand ethical behaviour or moral standards especially when doing things that have not been given rules.

LANGUAGE AND SPEECH DEVELOPMENT

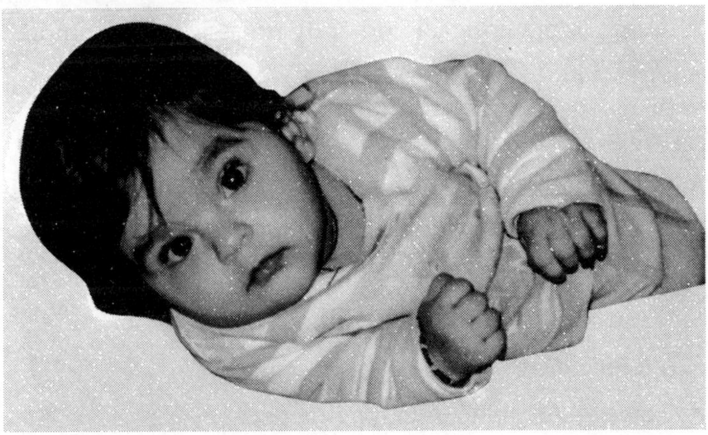

Two Year Old

- Realizes language is effective for getting desired responses.
- Uses fifty to three-hundred words; vocabulary continuously increasing.
- Has broken the linguistic code; in other words, much of a two-year-old's talk has meaning to him or her.
- Receptive language is more developed than expressive language; most two-year olds understand significantly more than they can talk about.

- Refers to self as “me” or sometimes “I” rather than by name: “Me go bye-bye”; has no trouble verbalizing “mine.”
- Utters three- and four-word statements; uses conventional word order to form more complete sentences.
- Enjoys participating while being read to.
- Expresses negative statements by tacking on a negative word such as “no” or “not”: “Not more milk.”
- Speech is as much as 65 to 70 percent intelligible.
- Is able to verbalize needs.
- Uses some plurals.
- Some stammering and other dysfluencies are common.
- Asks a lot of questions.

Three Year Old

- Knows chief parts of body and should be able to indicate these if not name.
- Use pronouns I, you, me correctly.
- Knows at least three prepositions, usually in, on, under.
- Handles three word sentences easily.
- Is using some plurals and past tenses.
- Verbs begin to predominate.
- Able to reason out such questions as “what must you do when you are sleepy, hungry, cool, or thirsty?”
- Should be able to give his sex, name, age.
- Should not be expected to answer all questions even though he understands what is expected.
- Relates his experiences so that they can be followed with reason
- About 90% of what child says should be intelligible.
- Has in the neighbourhood of 900-1000 words.

- Understands most simple questions dealing with his environment and activities.

Four Year Old

- Answers “Whose?”, “Who?”, “Why?”, and “How many?”
- Uses possessives consistently: “hers,” “theirs,” “babies.”
- Uses the prepositions “on,” “in” and “under.”
- Produces elaborate sentence structures: “The cat ran under the table before I could see.”
- Speech is almost entirely intelligible.
- Begins to use the past tense of verbs correctly: “Mommy closed the door,” “Daddy went to work.”
- Changes tone of voice and sentence structure to adapt to listener’s level of understanding. Example - To Mother, “Did the baby drink all of his milk?”
- States first and last name, gender, siblings’ names, and sometimes own telephone number.
- Answers appropriately when asked what to do if tired, cold, or hungry. Recites and sings simple songs like mangoes and rhymes.
- Refers to activities, events, objects and people that are not present.

Five Year Old

- Tells a familiar story while looking at pictures in a book.
- Defines simple words by function: a ball is to bounce; a bed is to sleep in.
- Identifies and names four to eight colours.
- Recognizes the humour in simple jokes; makes up jokes and riddles.
- Speech is almost entirely grammatically correct.

- Answers telephone appropriately; calls person to phone or takes a brief message.
- Produces sentences with five to seven words; much longer sentences are not unusual.
- States the name of own city or town, birthday and parents' names.
- Vocabulary of 1,500 words plus.
- Uses past-tense inflection (-ed) appropriately to mark regular verbs: "jumped," "rained," "washed
- Uses past tense of irregular verbs consistently: "went," "caught," "swam."
- Uses "would" and "could" appropriately.

Six Year Old

- Talks a lot.
- Can identify right and left hands fairly consistently.
- Loves telling jokes and riddles; often, the humor is far from subtle.
- Arrives at some understanding about death and dying; expresses fear that parents may die.
- Uses appropriate verb tenses, word order and sentence structure.
- Learns 5 to 10 words a day; vocabulary of 10,000–14,000.
- Able to carry on adult-like conversations; asks many questions.
- Enthusiastic and inquisitive about surroundings and everyday events.

CHALLENGING BEHAVIOUR OF CHILDREN

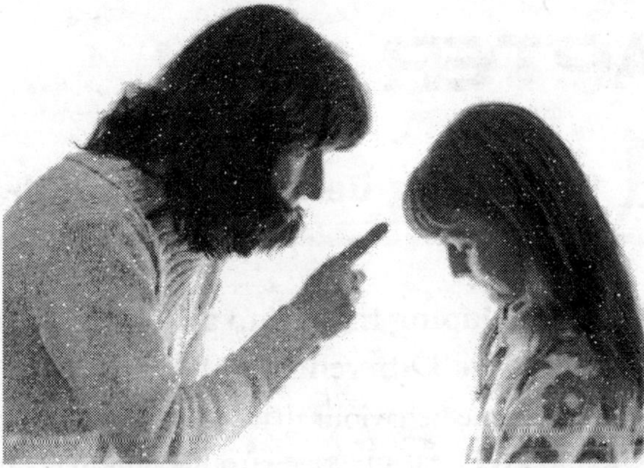

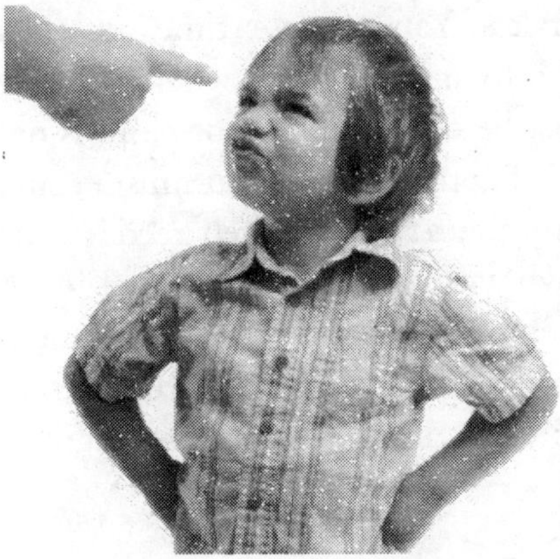

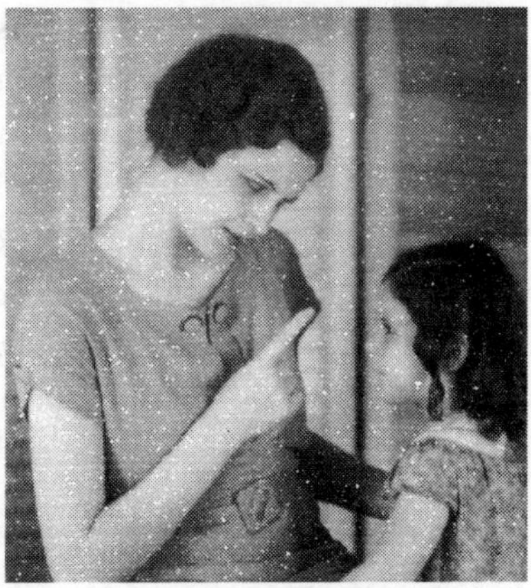

Dont Scold Child, give him Calm Environment

CHAPTER 31 Challenging Behaviour of Children

Your Role in Developing them into a Good Human Being: All Children Behave Differently

There may be some behaviour that you want to change. Always be consistent and give clear messages. Young children can be easily confused by change, support them to make these changes and don't punish them if they make mistakes. You can use 'time out' as a discipline by putting your child into another room where they are safe. Before you do this you must be certain that your child is old enough to understand why this is happening and you must ensure you keep the time reasonable. Sometimes what children need is 'time in'–some special time on their own with a parent or caregiver when you can do something that they enjoy and when you can comment on good behaviour. If they continue their bad behaviour tell the child that the special time is over and it can continue when they begin to behave better.

DISCIPLINING THE CHILD

When you Discipline your young Child, you should Remember that

- You may have to repeat that this behaviour is not OK over and over again
- This should be teaching and not punishment
- Your child needs to hear that it is the behaviour, not them, that you don't like

While the Child is Aggressive

If Your Child is Aggressive it Helps if you

- have a clear rule that violence or aggression isn't acceptable in your family or with you (and ensure that adults follow this rule too)
- never reward aggressive or violent behaviour – always have a negative consequence, such as time out or no TV
- encourage them to talk about things, not just hit out
- check out the TV programmes they're watching and monitor their viewing patterns and times
- praise the good things they do
- teach asking and negotiation and model these skills yourself
- reward them for changes in their behaviour

While the Child is Telling Lies

If you are Worried about Lies, you should Remember that

- remember that a child doesn't have the same idea of truth as an adult
- be truthful yourself – your child will pick up on any 'white lies' and not see any difference between these and a more serious kind
- they may just be fantasising and talking about something they wish was true
- reward them when they do tell the truth, even if it was something you didn't want to hear

While the Child is wetting Bed

Many children wet the bed and some boys do take longer than is considered 'normal' to grow out of this. Never punish your child for wetting the bed. You can try rewards for dry nights but it is a developmental stage that most children will pass through – some just take longer than others. Get help if you are concerned.

While the Child is does not Cooperate

If your Child doesn't Cooperate with your Directions it Helps if you

- are telling and not asking them to do something
- give specific instructions
- are not giving them too many tasks at once
- don't get caught up in discussions or arguments about what you want the child to do.

Reform: While the child cooperates

Give a clear instruction

Wait 5 to 20 seconds for your child to co-operate

If he does;

Give specific praise and be very enthusiastic

Reward the good behaviour with positive attention

When your child cooperates regularly, acknowledge this with a 'thank you'

If they don't:

Repeat your instruction

If possible, make it firmer and shorter

If they cooperate the second time, praise this behaviour

If they don't cooperate, use a consequence, such as time out or turning off the TV

Encouragement for Good Behaviour

You can encourage your child to cooperate if you:

- add a reward to the instruction but give the instruction first – 'put on your pyjamas and I'll read you a story'
- find out what they would prefer to be doing – if your child doesn't want to eat their dinner, then suggest a bath or a game afterwards
- Give them simple tasks with a limited choice – 'what will you put away, the cars or the blocks?'
- Help them with the things you want them to do – such as putting away the cars while they pack up their blocks.

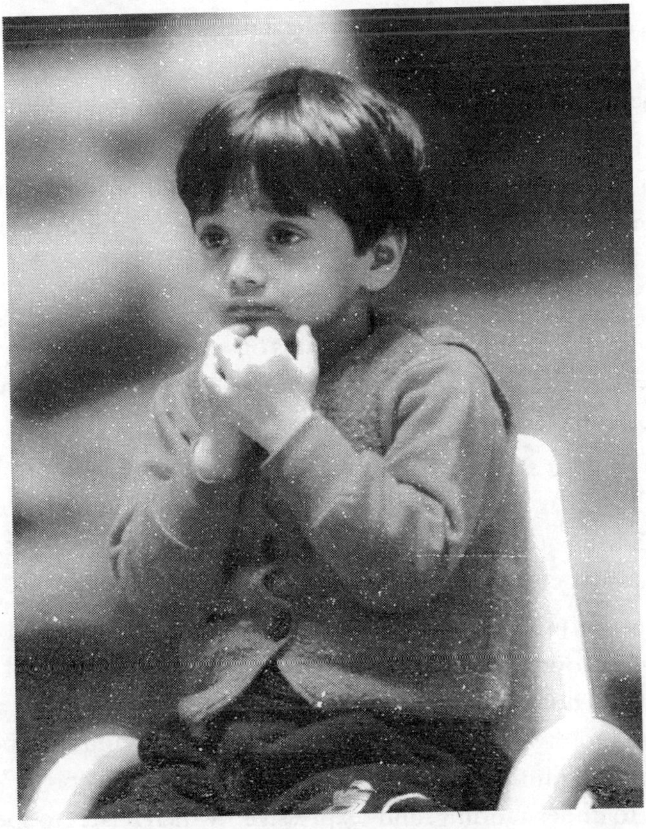

CHAPTER 32 Developmental Delay in Children

As you watch your child grow, it helps to remember that each child develops at his or her own pace and the range of normal is quite wide. However, it is helpful to be aware of potential developmental delays in children. These delays are significant lags in one or more areas of emotional, mental, or physical growth. If your child experiences a delay, early treatment is the best way to help him or her make progress or even to catch up.

In most children, delays in mental and physical development will improve. Some have significant delays — developmental delays — that may indicate possible future learning disabilities.

As you watch your child grow and anticipate his milestones, it's natural to whether his development is on track (*For example* you feel that "Shouldn't he be crawling by now?" But chances are that he'll develop just fine, on his own timeline.

In most instances, babies reach each developmental milestone like rolling over, sitting, walking and talking right around the expected time, and if not, they catch up soon. If is important if your baby does have a genuine developmental delay.

Doctors use the term 'Developmental delay' when a child doesn't reach developmental milestones within the broad range of what's considered normal. The delay might be in one or more areas: Gross and fine motor skills such as sitting-up and grasping and manipulating objects, communication and language skills both "receptive," which relates to understanding, and "expressive," which relates to speaking, self-help skills like toilet training and dressing and social skills such as making eye contact and playing with others.

So, *for example*, one 9-month-old may have very advanced motor skills because she loves to explore and interact through movement but not spend much time jabbering, while another baby the same age may be playing with syllables and calling you "mama" but be less adept at motor skills. "What's most important to track is that the child is making forward progress in all domains".

Various studies have reported that 10 to 15 percent of children under the age of 3 had a developmental delay, such as difficulty learning, communicating, playing, or performing physical activities or practical skills.

Early intervention can make a huge difference for many children with developmental delays, yet one study found that only about 3 percent of kids were getting appropriate attention. That's why it's important for you to speak up if you suspect your child has a developmental delay.

Kinds of Problems

Most parents are pretty sensitive to the age at which their baby reaches **gross motor skill** milestones, like crawling and walking – and whether these achievements are considered "early" or "late." But you might also pick up on your child's finer motor skills, like his ability to pick up peas from his highchair tray or to pass a toy from one hand to another.

In the **language arena**, you might notice that your baby has difficulty with receptive language (understanding the meanings of words and sentences) or with expressive language (expressing ideas in words). Or he might have trouble with what doctors call "communicative intent" – the ability to express himself by pointing, imitating and making sounds.

It's a good idea to familiarize yourself with the normal timeline for developing **cognitive and physical skills**, so you can use it as a general guideline. That way you'll know that by 3 or 4 months most babies can grasp and reach for objects, *for example*, and around 9 months most can stand while holding on to something. You'll see that at about 9 months most babies understand the concept of object permanence (that an object still exists, even when they can't see it), and that by their first birthday most children can communicate their desires.

Keep in mind that **if your child was born prematurely**, he might sometimes need a bit more time than other kids his age to reach the various developmental stages. Most doctors assess a preterm child's development against the time he should have been born (his due date rather than his actual birth date) and evaluate his skills accordingly until his second or third birthday.

CAUSES OF DEVELOPMENTAL DELAY

What is Developmental Delay?

Developmental Delay is when your child does not reach his developmental milestones at the expected times. It is an *ongoing major or minor delay in the process of development*. If your child is temporarily lagging behind, that is not called developmental delay. Delay can occur in one or many areas—*for example*, gross or fine motor, language, social, or thinking skills.

Developmental Delay is most often a diagnosis made by a doctor based on strict guidelines. Usually, though, the parent is the first to notice that their child is not progressing at the same rate as other children the same age. If you think your child may be "slow," or "seems behind," talk with your child's doctor about it. In some cases, your paediatrician might pick up a delay during an office visit.

The first three years of a child's life are an amazing time of development...and what happens during those years stays with a child for a lifetime. That's why it's so important to watch for signs of delays in development, and to get help if you suspect problems. The sooner a delayed child gets early intervention, the better their progress will be. *So, if you have concerns, act early.*

Causes of Developmental Delay

Developmental delay can have many different causes, such as genetic causes (like Down syndrome) , or complications of pregnancy and birth (like prematurity or infections). Often, however, the specific cause is unknown. Some causes can be easily reversed if caught early enough, such as hearing loss from chronic ear infections, or lead poisoning.

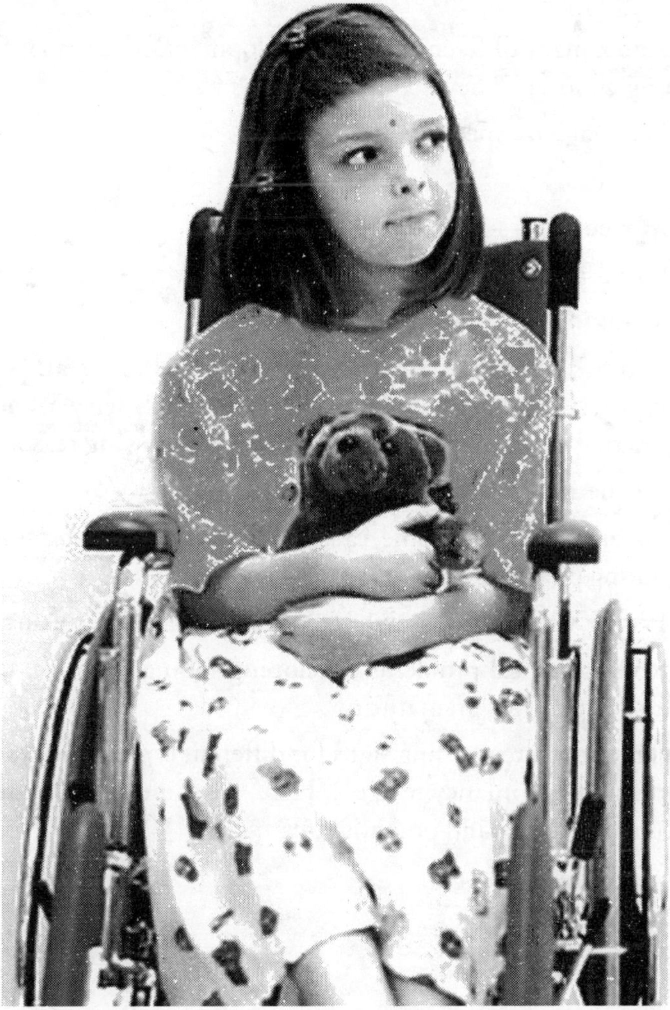

CHAPTER 33 Types of Developmental Delays in Children

There are many different types of developmental delays in infants and young children. They include problems with:

- **Language or speech**
- **Vision**
- **Movement — motor skills**
- **Social and emotional skills**
- **Thinking — cognitive skills**

Sometimes, a delay occurs in many or all of these areas. When that happens, it is called "global developmental delay." Global developmental delay may occur for any of the following reasons:

- A genetic defect, such as Down syndrome
- Foetus alcohol syndrome, caused by a mother drinking alcohol during pregnancy
- Fragile X syndrome, an inherited type of cognitive impairment
- Severe medical problems developing soon after birth, often associated with prematurity

What follows are warning signs for different types of delays that may show up from infancy to age 2. Here, are some of the causes of developmental delays and potential treatments.

Language and Speech Developmental Delays

Speech delay in toddlers is common. In fact, language and speech problems are the most common type of developmental delay. Speech refers to verbal expression, including the way words are formed. Language is a broader system of expressing and receiving information, such as being able to understand directions.

Possible causes: A variety of problems may cause language and speech delays, including:

- a learning disability
- hearing loss, which may occur in children who have severe middle ear infections or occur as a result of certain medications, trauma, or genetic disorders
- exposure to more than one language — which can cause mild delays in toddlers but not delays by the time they reach school age
- a problem with the muscles controlling speech — a disorder called dysarthria
- autism spectrum disorders — a group of neurological disorders that may involve impaired communication as well as impaired social interaction and cognitive skills

Types of Treatment

If your child's doctor suspects a speech delay problem, seek an evaluation by a speech-language pathologist. This specialist may test your child's hearing and use speech therapy with your child. The specialist or doctor may also suggest that you:

- communicate more with your child — talk, sing, and encourage repetition
- read daily to your child
- reinforce speech and language throughout the day
- get treatment for middle ear infections

Warning Signs of Speech or Language Delays

Contact your child's doctor if your child has any of the following signs at the age that's indicated. In addition, watch for any loss of skills that have already been learned. These are just warnings; you can wait for 2-3 months. Sometimes some children learn may slow.

By 3 to 4 months, contact the doctor if your child:

- does not respond to loud noises
- does not babble
- begins babbling but does not try to imitate sounds (by 4 months)

By 7 months, contact the doctor if your child:

- does not respond to sounds

By 1 year, contact the doctor if your child:

- does not use any single words (like "mama")

By 2 years, contact the doctor if your child:

- does not use speech to communicate more than immediate needs
- cannot speak at least 15 words
- does not use two-word phrases without repetition; can only imitate speech

Types of Treatment

If your child's doctor suspects a speech delay problem, seek an evaluation by a speech-language pathologist. This specialist may test your child's hearing and use speech therapy with your child. The specialist or doctor may also suggest that you:

- communicate more with your child — talk, sing and encourage repetition

- read daily to your child
- reinforce speech and language throughout the day
- get treatment for middle ear infections

VISION DEVELOPMENTAL DELAYS IN CHILDREN

Until 6 months, a newborn's vision is normally blurry. Then it improves as the child begins to coordinate sight in both eyes. However, sometimes this does not happen or other vision problems show up.

Possible causes of Vision Delays

Refractive errors, such as nearsightedness and farsightedness, are common in children. Other eye problems include:

- amblyopic (lazy eye), poor vision in one eye
- infantile cataracts — a clouding of the eye's lens — or another inherited problem (these problems are rare)
- retinopathy of prematurity, an eye disease that sometimes affects premature infants
- strabismus — also called cross eyed — eyes that turn in, out, up, or down

Types of Treatment

If your child's doctor suspects a speech delay problem, seek an evaluation by a speech-language pathologist. This specialist may test your child's hearing and use speech therapy with your child. The specialist or doctor may also suggest that you:

- communicate more with your child — talk, sing, and encourage repetition
- read daily to your child
- reinforce speech and language throughout the day
- get treatment for middle ear infections

Warning Signs of Vision Problems

You should contact your doctor if your child has any of the following signs at the age that's indicated. In addition, watch for any loss of skills that have already been learned.

By 3 months, contact the doctor if your child:

- does not notice hands (by 2 months)
- does not follow moving objects with his or her eyes
- has trouble moving one or both eyes in all directions
- crosses eyes most of the time

By 6 months, contact the doctor if your child:

- has one or both eyes turning in or out all the time
- does not follow near objects (1 foot away) or far objects (6 feet away) with both eyes
- experiences constant tearing, eye drainage, or sensitivity to light

Types of Treatment Delays

If your child's doctor notes any problems, the doctor may refer your child to an ophthalmologist for further evaluation.

Motor Skill Developmental Delays in Children

Developmental delays may be related to problems with gross motor skills, such as crawling or walking, or fine motor skills, such as using fingers to grasp a spoon.

Possible causes of Motor Skill Delays

Children who are born prematurely may not develop muscles at the same rate as other children.

Children who have been institutionalized, **lacked stimulation** at young ages, or have **autism** may have sensory integration dysfunction. This complex disorder has been thought to cause a variety of problems with the senses, including:

- extreme reactions to touch, textures, or pain
- fearful reactions to ordinary movements or an excessive need to seek out sensory input such as, *for example*, by rocking, spinning, or hand-flapping
- problems planning and coordinating movement

Other **possible causes** of motor delays include:

- cerebral palsy, a condition caused by brain damage near the time of birth

- ataxia, a genetic defect that impairs muscle coordination
- cognitive delays
- problems with vision
- sympathy, a disease of the muscles
- spina bifida, a genetic condition causing partial or total paralysis of the lower part of the body

Warning Signs of Motor Skill Delays

Contact your child's doctor if your child has any of the following signs at the age that's indicated. In addition, watch for any loss of skills that have already been learned.

By 3 to 4 months, contact the doctor if your child:

- does not support his or her head well
- does not reach for, grasp, or hold objects
- does not push down with legs when his or her feet are placed on a firm surface (by 4 months)
- does not bring objects to his or her mouth (by 4 months)

By 7 months, contact the doctor if your child:

- flops his or her head when pulled into a sitting position
- has stiff and tight or very floppy muscles
- reaches with one hand only or does not actively reach for objects
- doesn't roll over in either direction (by 5 months)
- has trouble getting objects to his or her mouth
- cannot sit up without help (by 7 months)
- does not bear weight on his or her legs when you pull him or her up to a standing position

By 1 year, contact the doctor if your child:

- does not crawl
- drags one side of his or her body while crawling
- cannot stand when supported

By 2 years, contact the doctor if your child:

- cannot walk (by 18 months)

- does not develop a heel-to-toe walking pattern or walks only on toes
- cannot push a wheeled toy

COGNITIVE DEVELOPMENTAL DELAYS IN CHILDREN

Possible Causes

Problems with thinking, or cognitive delays, may occur due to one or more of these reasons:

- genetic defects
- exposure to something harmful in the environment, such as a toxin
- significant medical problems soon after birth
- severe newborn medical problems
- pervasive developmental disorder
- a wide range of different learning disabilities
- exposure to alcohol or toxins before birth or afterward, including lead poisoning
- Down syndrome and other genetic disorders
- institutionalization or neglect during infancy or early childhood

Treatment for Cognitive Delays

As with most types of developmental delays, early treatment can make a big difference in the progress your child makes. Educational intervention can help your child develop specific cognitive skills. Educators and therapists may also recommend specific steps you can take at home to help your child.

Warning Signs of Cognitive Delays

You should contact your child's doctor if your child has any of the following signs at the age that's indicated. In addition, watch for any loss of skills that have already been learned.

By 1 year, contact the doctor if your child:

- does not search for objects that are hidden while he or she watches

- does not use gestures, such as waving
- does not point to objects or pictures

By 2 years, contact the doctor if your child:

- does not know the function of common objects, such as a hairbrush, telephone, or spoon
- does not follow simple instructions
- does not imitate actions or words

Treatment for Cognitive Delays

As with most types of developmental delays, early treatment can make a big difference in the progress your child makes. Educational intervention can help your child develop specific cognitive skills. Educators and therapists may also recommend specific steps you can take at home to help your child.

Remember: There is a wide range of normal development in children. Most developmental delays in children are not serious and children eventually catch up. Even children who do have serious delays can make big improvements when treatment begins as early as possible. If you have any doubts, talk to your child's health care provider.

SOCIAL AND EMOTIONAL DEVELOPMENTAL DELAYS IN CHILDREN

Children may experience problems interacting with adults or other children, called social and/or emotional developmental delays. Usually these problems show up before a child begins school.

Possible causes: Some causes of social and emotional delays include:

- neglect from early institutionalization or parental neglect
- ineffective parenting or attachment problems
- cognitive delays

Another common cause of social and emotional developmental delays is Pervasive Developmental Disorder (PDD). This group of disorders also causes communication problems ranging from mild to severe. PDD includes:

- autism, a complex yet common disorder
- Asperser's syndrome
- childhood disintegrative disorder
- Rhett syndrome

Treatment: There is no known cure for PDD. However, treatment may include:

- special types of behavioural and skill-oriented therapy
- medication if therapies do not work

As with most types of delays, early treatment can make a big difference in the progress your child makes. Depending upon the diagnosis, treatment may also include play therapy or steps to aid attachment between parent and child.

Warning Signs of Social or Emotional Delays

You should contact your child's doctor if your child has any of the following signs at the age that's indicated. In addition, watch for any loss of skills that have already been learned.

By 3 months, contact the doctor if your child:

- does not smile at people
- does not pay attention to new faces, or seems frightened by them

By 7 months, contact the doctor if your child:

- refuses to cuddle
- shows no affection for parents or caregivers
- does not smile without prompting (by 5 months)
- cannot be comforted at night (after 5 months)
- shows no enjoyment around people
- does not laugh or squeal (by 6 months)

By 1 year, contact the doctor if your child:

- shows no back-and-forth sharing of sounds, smiles, or facial expressions (at 9 months)
- shows no back-and-forth gestures, such as waving, reaching, or pointing

CHAPTER 34 6 Year Old Child's Development

You Notice that your 6 Year Old will Mature Emotionally

Like many phases of child development, the period **of 6-year-old development** is characterized by contradictions. A 6-year-old child will have his foot more firmly in the big-kid years. At the same time, he will still experience the insecurity that comes from stepping more into the big wide world without the constant comfort of mom and dad. As he increasingly experiences school, play dates, birthday parties, and other activities without a parent, he may want and need more attention and comfort at home.

Emotional Awareness of Child

Six-year-olds will become more aware of emotions — both their own as well as those of others. They may understand sophisticated concepts such as how to be careful about not hurting someone's feelings by saying something critical about them directly to that person.

Independence

Six-year-olds are increasingly engaging in activities without their parents. But as they transition toward increasing independence, they will rely more on the security of home, routines, parents, and friends. Predictable routines such as nighttimes' rituals, after-school activities and regular play dates with friends will be important for 6-year-olds; for them, these regular activities and relationships will provide the security they need as they encounter unfamiliar challenges and experiences.

Children this age may also increasingly express a desire to choose their own clothes, wash themselves and comb their own hair. Parents can help encourage this independent self-care and offer some guidance and help (by letting kids wash themselves and "helping" at the end or suggesting a sweater and tights if it's too cold to go to school in just a favourite frilly skirt, for instance).

Confidence and Insecurity of Child

For many 6-year-old children of child, the centre of the universe will, for all intents and purposes, still be them. Six-year-olds will regale others with stories about themselves and will naturally expect others to be as interested in them as they are. They will be proud of their accomplishments and talents and will want to share their artwork, physical abilities and other things about themselves that they feel make them stand out and be special. It will be up to parents to guide and teach them about the fine line **between confidence and boasting.**

At the same time, they will feel insecure and will want praise from others. Six-year-olds may want to do things perfectly, and may be hard on themselves if their performance isn't as good as they wanted it to be (For example if they lose at a game. They will want to fit in and will want their friends at school to approve of the things they do. Six-year-olds may have a hard time accepting criticism and may be more sensitive to discipline.

Much of this insecurity will stem from a 6-year-old's natural move toward independence. Parents can help by being aware of this push and pull, and can help their child feel better about forging ahead more on their own by providing a comforting atmosphere at home where kids can feel secure in daily routines and reassurances of love and understanding.

Inflexibility and Preferences

Six-year-olds will often see things as black and white and will express strong opinions about things. They may go from elation about something to absolute unhappiness if something doesn't go their way. They may see something as good and something else as bad and will have trouble seeing the middle ground.

This kind of thinking is common for 6-year-olds, who are trying to organize and categorize the world around them. Pigeon-holing something into a category can help 6-year-olds make sense of it, and it can help them feel like they can master unknown and new experiences. Parents can help by gently steering kids toward nuanced thinking, by suggesting that they see things from other points of view — a skill they will naturally acquire as they grow older.

Privacy

Six-year-olds may begin to express a desire for privacy when they dress or undress (although many will still enjoy bath time with a parent close by and will ask mother or father to wash their hair). Children this age may begin to get curious about their own bodies, gender and sex and you can expect questions about where babies come from.

Behaviour and Daily Routines

As 6-year-old children increasingly move toward independence, engaging in activities without mother and father and socializing with friends, such as at birthday parties or play ground, routines at home will change and take on a greater significance.

Six-year-old children, like adults are individuals, with distinct interests, abilities and experiences. It's not possible to say what all 6-year-olds are like; here is a general overview of what you can expect.

Six-year-old children will be able to ready, willing and able to handle more responsibilities, both at home and at school. Children this age can be given age-appropriate activities. At school, 6-year-olds will be able to handle acting as line monitors or helping the teacher hand out assignment sheets.

Diet

Parents of 6-year-olds can set many healthy habits and patterns such as choosing healthy foods, sitting down to dinner together as a family and establishing good table manners — skills that will become important for children to have in the years to come.

Parents of 6-year-old children can expect their kids to be interested in dinner conversation and be able to have the attention span and self-control to sit for most of the meal. This can be an ideal age to reinforce those table manners that 6-year-olds may not have been able to consistently put into practice when they were younger.

Some 6-year-olds may continue to hold on to their picky eating habits while others may one day decide to venture into new foods and flavours (possibly inspired by friends and peers from school). Either way, this will be an excellent age for parents to begin steering kids into healthy eating habits. They can offer and encourage kids to try new dishes — ideally ones comprised of healthy vegetables.

One thing parents may want to watch out for is children being influenced by their peers to want unhealthy foods such as soda, candy, and other junk food. Talk about how healthy foods, such as fruits, vegetables, and low fat milk, are "growing" food and consistently reinforce the message that junk food is only for occasional treats.

Sleep

Children this age need anywhere between 10 to 12 hours of sleep at night, although some kids may need less or more, depending on individual requirements. The challenge for parents, though, will be how to fit in homework, after-school play dates and activities and family time after school so that kids go to bed on time. One way might be to filter out the things that can compete for a child's attention, such as TV and videogames and restrict such activities to weekends.

Night time routines and good sleep habits will become more significant as children fall into school routines, and need to be well-rested and ready for school in the mornings. Many 6-year-olds are learning to read, but will still enjoy being read to at bedtime. If he's able and interested, you can take turns reading to each other.

Discipline and Behaviour

As 6-year-old children become more independent and increasingly begin to want more control over the things that affect them such as what they wear and eat or how they spend their time, behaviour problems can sometimes surface. They may naturally try to test limits and boundaries as they explore their newly-developing identities as bigger kids. For parents, this can mean dealing more with typical 6-year-old behaviour problems such as defiance or back talk.

At the same time, 6-year-olds are still young children who haven't yet left behaviours such as tantrums and whining behind them. Typical of this age, parents can expect to see some regressive behaviour alternating with more "big-kid" abilities.

With love and consistent discipline and guidance, parents can help their 6-year-old child weather the changes that can affect behaviour. By becoming patient and giving your child room to make mistakes even as you are clear about your expectations for good behaviour, you will help your child overcome behaviour problems at home and at school.

7 Year Old Child's Development

CHAPTER 35 7 Year Old Child's Development

For 7-year-old children, independence is not just about dressing themselves or brushing their own teeth anymore. Many 7-year-olds may enjoy making significant decisions, such as choosing extracurricular activities or taking on more responsibilities at school and at home. They are in a transitional phase.

Here, are some milestones parents can generally expect to see in a 7-year-old. Some children may experience these phases of development sooner while others hit them later — there is no one formula that fits all children.

Physical Development

For a 7-year-old child, physical development will be more about refinement than major changes. Seven-year-olds will continue to grow into long-limbed and lanky versions of their former chubby preschooler selves as their motor skills become more precise. Seven-year-old children will also develop better coordination and balance.

Emotional Development

In this age emotional development will become noticeable as they become better at handling the unexpected and weathering changes. Seven-year-old children may still lack the self-control of, say, a middle-scholar, but 7-year-olds will be much more adept at handling transitions and surprises than younger children. Read about 7-year-old emotional development.

Social Development

Social networks and friendships are important to 7-year-old children, who are continuing to form bonds with peers, teachers, and teammates. Children of this age will begin to care more about the opinions and thoughts of other people; the downside of this natural phase of child development is an increased susceptibility to peer pressure. Seven-year-old children will also continue to develop empathy and a strong sense of morals and fairness.

Cognitive Development

7 year-old children are curious about the world around them. They will ask questions and seek answers about the things they encounter and the people they meet and will take pride in sharing what they know. They will display a formidable sense of adventure and thirst for information and will love being mentors to younger siblings and other children as they show off their newfound knowledge and skills.

Behaviour

Parenting a 7-year-old child is less about close supervision and more about guidance and reminders. Seven-year-old children are growing more self-sufficient and are better able to take care of their own daily routines. Seven-year-old children may also express an increasing desire to make more decisions and choices for themselves. Read about 7-year-old behaviour and daily routines.

CHAPTER 36 8 Year Old Child's Development

Eight-year-old's behaviour and daily routines are shaped by unique, individual tastes, interests and personalities. Parents and other significant adults in an 8-year-old child's life should keep in mind the importance of being good role models since this is a time when children are figuring out the world and who they are and how they fit into it. Read about 8-year-old child behaviour and daily routines.

Physical and Motor Development

Physical development will continue to be more about refinement of skills, co-ordination and muscle control rather than huge changes and leaps in development. Eight-year-old children who have natural athletic ability may show their skills at this developmental stage as physical skills become more precise and accurate.

Emotional Development

Eight-year-old emotional development may be growing at a deeper level than in younger years, and an 8-year-old may show more sophisticated and complex emotions and interactions. For instance, an 8-year-old may mask true thoughts or emotions to spare someone else's feelings or work through a problem without an adult's close supervision or intervention.

Cognitive Development

Children at this stage will be able to pay attention for longer periods of time. You can expect 8-year-old kids to be able to concentrate on an activity for up to an hour or more. Eight-year-olds will also be able to think more critically and express opinions using more complex and sophisticated vocabulary and language skills.

Social Development

These children love being a part of sports teams and other social groups, and will enjoy close friendships with select friends. Eight-year-old children generally love going to school and will count on and value relationships with friends and classmates. Parents of 8-year-olds can face the problems such as school refusal, learning difficulties or being bullied at school if their child expresses unhappiness about school or classmates.

Middle Childhood: Care for 6-8 Years of Age

CHAPTER 37 Middle Childhood: Care for 6-8 Years of Age

Middle childhood brings many changes in a child's life. By this time, children can dress themselves, catch a ball more easily using only their hands and tie their shoes. Having independence from family becomes more important now. Children come to regular contact with the larger world. Friendships become more and more important. Physical, social and mental skills develop quickly at this time. This is a critical time for children to develop confidence in all areas of life, such as through friends, schoolwork and sports.

Emotional/Social/Cognitive Changes

Children in this age group might

- Show more independence from parents and family.
- Want to be liked and accepted by friends.
- Pay more attention to friendships and teamwork.
- Understand more about his or her place in the world.
- Have less focus on one's self and more concern for others.
- Learn better ways to describe experiences and talk about thoughts and feelings.
- Show rapid development of mental skills.

Positive Parenting Tip Sheet

Positive parenting tips for right development

Following are some things you, as a parent, can do to help your child during this time:

- Talk with your child about school, friends, and things he/she likes.

- Show affection for your child. Recognize his/her accomplishments.
- Help your child develop a sense of responsibility—ask him/her to help with little household tasks according to your home.
- Help your child set her own achievable goals—she'll learn to take pride in herself and rely less on approval or reward from others.
- Talk with your child about respecting others. Encourage him to help people in need.
- Support your child in taking on new challenges. Encourage her to solve problems, such as a disagreement with another child, on his/her own.
- Get involved with your child's school. Meet the teachers and staff and get to understand their learning goals and how you and the school can work together to help your child do well.
- Do fun things together as a family, such as playing games, reading, and going to events in your community.
- Encourage your child to join school and community groups, such as a team sports, or to take advantage of volunteer opportunities.
- Praise your child for good behaviour. It's best to focus praise more on what your child does than on traits he/she can't change.
- Use discipline to guide and protect your child, rather than punishment to make him feel bad about himself. Follow up any discussion about what *not* to do with a discussion of what *to* do instead.
- Make clear rules and stick to them, such as how long your child can watch TV or when she has to go to bed. Be clear about what behaviour is okay and what is not okay.
- Help your child learn patience by letting others go first or by finishing a task before going out to play. Encourage him/her to think about possible consequences before acting.

CHAPTER 38 Nine-Year-Old Child's Development

These children are in a child development period of major transition as they stand on the cusp of adolescence. In many ways, 9-year-olds are still young children; but they are becoming much more independent and are developmentally mature enough to handle many responsibilities and situations with minimal adult intervention.

Physical Development

9-year-old children are on the cusp of adolescence. This is a major phase of child development in which they can expect many physical, emotional, and other changes. Many 9-year-old children will have stronger and smoother muscle control, be able to handle much of their hygiene and personal care by themselves. They may experience the beginnings of puberty. Children of this age may also be more susceptible to body image issues.

Emotional Development

At the age of 9, many children are more emotionally mature, and are better able to handle conflicts and frustrations. These children will be more independent, and will be emotionally more ready to socialize without their parents. They have a strong desire to belong to a group and to fit in and may be more susceptible to peer influence and peer pressure. They may be more moody. They feel more stress and pressure, and will rely upon the support and love provided by parents.

Cognitive Development

9-year-old children are incredibly curious about the world around them, and may want to research topics that interest them. They have longer attention spans and will tend to spend lots of time on activities and subjects that they are excited about. They will be able to think critically, and may want to share their opinions about things. They will like to read and write increasingly more complicated texts. They will like to learn how to work with multiple digits, geometry, and data organization in math.

Social Development

The social world of the 9-year-old child is opening up more than ever before. At 9, many children consider friendships to be very important, and they may even have adult role models who are not their mother and father, such as a coach or a film hero/heroine or a teacher. Peer pressure may become an issue at this age and many children will have a strong sense of fairness and right and wrong. Children may also become more socially conscious. Some children at this age become interested in bettering the world and helping others.

Behaviour

Many 9-year-old children are becoming more interested in helping make major decisions that affect the family, and are capable of taking on more responsibilities around the house. Children this age also tend to want a certain amount of organization and may want to keep track of their activities and schedules. Some children are careless and some carefree at this age.

At 9, many children are increasingly expanding their social circles to include more people outside their mother or father. At the same time, 9-year-old children still need and want the security of their relationship with their parents and some are greatly influenced by their parents.

9 years olds are emotionally mature

CHAPTER 39 10 Year Old Child's Development

Parents should always remember that it is a fact that all children don't experience the same development at certain age. There is difference in girls and boys developments also.

Ten-year-old children experience a natural need to have some distance from parents and family and are gravitating toward more social activities with peers. For parents who are used to being the center of their child's universe, this can be somewhat disheartening.

The important thing to remember is that while it's normal for 10-year-olds to have more independence, they will still need and want guidance and support from parents. A child always needs supervision as he grows older, the role of a parent will change, rather than diminish at all time.

Independence

A 10-year-old may suddenly view something he'd previously believed or followed without question — such as, *for example*, eating meat — and declare that he now believes he should be a vegetarian. Or he could change his mind about a favourite sports team and choose something different instead.

You may see many changes in your 10-year-old child may be passing phases, or they may lead to long-term ways of life. Whatever the case may be, it's important for parents to try to support their child and make sure that they know their opinions are valued and listened to.

Parents can help nurture this growing sense of independence in their 10-year-old child by giving her/him extra responsibilities and more age-appropriate chores around the house. Parents can also try to respect their child's growing need to spend time away from family. At the same time, it is essential that parents of 10-year-olds always keep an eye on what their kids are doing, where they are going and with whom so that they know their children activities.

Friends

At this age, many children are more concerned about what their friends and classmates are wearing, what music they're listening to, and what new trends they're following. Many 10-year-olds will naturally feel a great desire to fit in. Having a good sense of self and confidence can be very important at this age. When children have strong and healthy self-esteem, they will be better equipped to handle any potential pressure from peers who might try to convince them to do things they don't feel are safe and healthy.

It's common for 10-year-olds to prefer friendships with children of their own gender but some prefer friendship with opposite gender. They may also have one or two best friends with whom they can enjoy a close relationship.

Children of this age are become more interested in their appearance and how they measure up against others their own age. Insecurities about physical appearance can crop up at this age, making it important for parents to in still a healthy sense of body image in their children. Parents can also make sure that their child practices healthy eating habits to help him/her stay in shape and stay healthy and strong.

You may also want to sign your child up for group sports to keep him/her in shape but feel like she's part of a team. Playing sports can also help boost your child's self esteem by helping him/her feel like she's contributing to a group effort and accomplishing goals, all while getting healthy and strong.

True Guidance

For 10-year-old child right and wrong should be defined very rigidly, and according to what she/he believes based on her experience. Some of this strong sense of morals and rules is tied to her/him growing sense of independence, as she/he forms her own opinions about the world around her and as she increasingly spends more time with friends and independent activities away from her/his family.

At home, 10-year-old children will still need guidance as they navigate problems and work through behavioural issues. It's a fact that 10-year-olds are still young children who may need disciplining from time to time as they figure out how to be the person they want to be and how to fit in with the ideals they develop as they grow.

Middle Childhood: Care for 9-11 Years of Age

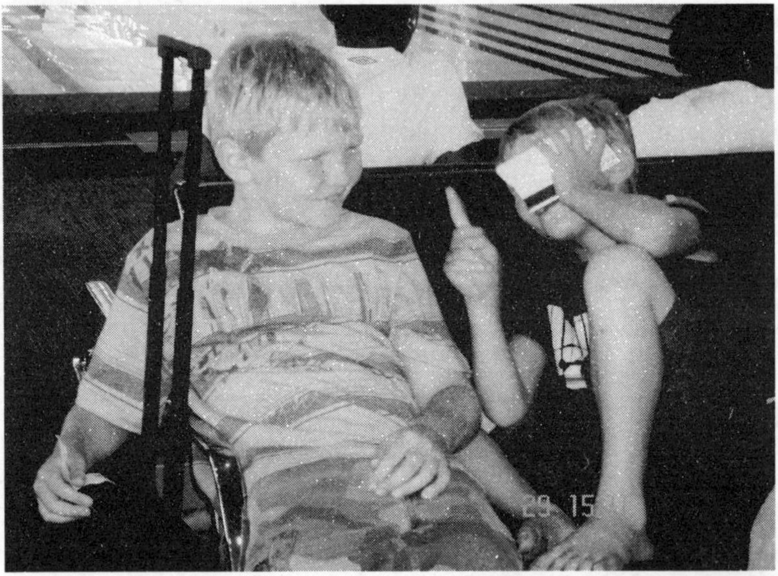

CHAPTER 40 Middle Childhood: Care for 9-11 Years of Age

Healthy friendships are very important to your child's development, but peer pressure can become strong during this time. Children who feel good about themselves are more able to resist negative peer pressure and make better choices for themselves. Your child's growing independence from the family and interest in friends might be obvious by now. This is an important time for children to gain a sense of responsibility alongwith their growing independence. Also, physical changes of puberty especially in girls might be showing by now.

Following is the information on emotional and social change of middle age children and on how children develop during middle childhood:

Children in this age group might:

- Experience more peer pressure.
- Become more aware of his or her body as puberty approaches. Body image and eating problems sometimes start around this age.
- Start to form stronger, more complex friendships and peer relationships. It becomes more emotionally important to have friends. In boys, puberty starts two years later in Indian atmosphere. Boys experience it at the age of 13-15 years.
- Begin to see the point of view of others more clearly.
- Have an increased attention span.
- Face more academic challenges at school.
- Become more independent from the family.

Positive Parenting Tip Sheet

Positive Parenting Tips for extra care and proper development of children.

Here, are some things you, as a parent, can do to help your child during this time:

- Be involved with your child's school. Go to school events; meet your child's teachers.
- Encourage your child to join school and community groups, such as a sports team, or to be a volunteer for a charity.
- Help your child develop his own sense of right and wrong. Talk with him/her about risky things friends might pressure him to do, like smoking or dangerous physical dares.
- Spend time with your child. Talk with her about her friends, her accomplishments and what challenges she or he will face.
- Talk with your child about respecting others. Encourage him/her to help people in need.
- At times meet the families of your child's friends.
- Help your child set his own goals. Encourage him to think about skills and abilities he would like to have and about how to develop them.
- Help your child develop a sense of responsibility—involve your child in household tasks like cleaning and cooking. Talk with your child about saving and spending money wisely.
- Make clear rules and stick to them. Talk with your child about what you expect from her. About behaviour when no adults are present. If you provide reasons for rules, it will help her/him to know what to do in most situations.
- Use discipline to guide and protect your child, instead of punishment to make him feel badly about himself.
- Encourage your child to read every day. Talk with him about his homework.

- Be affectionate and honest with your child and do things together as a family.
- Talk with your child about the normal physical and emotional changes of puberty.
- When using praise, help your child think about her own accomplishments. Saying "you must be proud of yourself" rather than simply "I'm proud of you" can encourage your child to make good choices when nobody is around to praise her.

CHAPTER 41

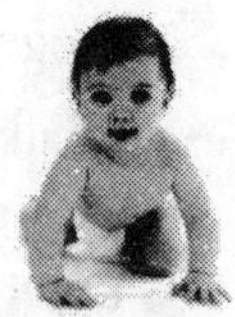

12-14 Years of Age: Young Teens

This is the age of many physical, mental, emotional and social changes. You find them totally changed at this time. Hormones change as puberty begins but many boys may not face such changes as they grow little bit slow and see these changes a little later.

Most boys grow facial and pubic hair and their voices deepen. Most girls grow pubic hair and breasts and start their period. They might be worried about these changes and how they are looked at by others. This also will be a time when your teen might face peer pressure to do adult experiences like to have sex or use drug set. Other challenges can be eating disorders, depression and family problems. At this age, teens make more of their own choices about friends, sports, studying and school. They become more independent, with their own personality and interests, although parents are still very important. In metropolitan and big cities child's physical, emotional development differs from those of small town and cities.

Specific changes and developments

Children in this age group might:

- Experience more moodiness.
- Show more concern about body image, looks and clothes.
- Show more interest in and influence by peer group.
- Focus on themselves; going back and forth between high expectations and lack of confidence.
- Develop eating problems.

- Feel stress from more challenging school work.
- Be better able to express feelings through talking.
- Develop a stronger sense of right and wrong.
- Have more ability for complex thought.
- Feel a lot of sadness or depression, which can lead to poor grades at school, alcohol or drug use, unsafe sex and other problems.
- Express less affection toward parents; sometimes might seem rude or short-tempered.

Positive parenting tips for your child's right development

Here, some things you can do to help your child's development during this time:

- Help your teen make healthy choices while encouraging him to make his own decisions.
- Respect your teen's opinions and take into account her thoughts and feelings. It is important that she/he knows you are listening to her/him.
- Meet and get to know your teen's friends.
- When there is a conflict, be clear about goals and expectations about getting good grades, keeping things clean and showing respect etc., but allow your teen input on how to reach those goals.
- Show an interest in your teen's school life.
- Be honest and direct with your teen when talking about sensitive subjects such as drugs, drinking, smoking and sex.®

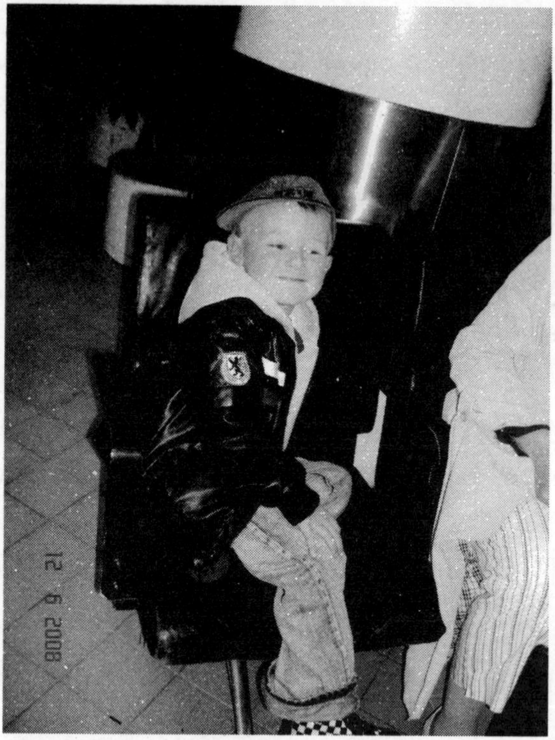
12 9 2008

Teenagers Behave in a Different Way

CHAPTER

42 15-17 Years of Age: Teenagers

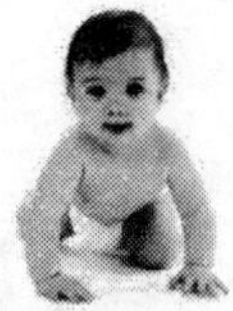

This is a time of many important changes in children's life. How you can see changes on teenagers think, feel and interact with others, and how their bodies grow. Most girls will be physically mature by now and most will have completed puberty. Boys might still be maturing physically during this time. Your teenage child might have concerns about his/her body size, shape, or weight. Eating disorders are very common, especially among girls.

During this time, your teen is developing his/her unique personality and opinions. Relationships with friends are still important, yet your teen will have other interests as he/she develops a more clear sense of who he/she is. This is also an important time to prepare for more independence and responsibility.

Specific changes (emotional and social) in development:

Children in this age group might:

- Show more independence from parents.
- Have more interest in the opposite sex.
- Like to spend less time with parents and more time with friends.
- Have a deeper capacity for caring and sharing and for developing more intimate relationships.
- Feel a lot of sadness or depression, which can lead to poor grades at school, unsafe sex, alcohol or drug use and other problems.
- Go through less conflict with parents.

- Be better able to give reasons for their own choices, including about what is right or wrong.
- Show more concern about future school or college and work plans.
- Learn more defined work and behaviour habits.

Positive parenting tips for teenager's development

Here, are some things you can do to help your teen during this time:

- Compliment your teen and celebrate his efforts and accomplishments.
- If your teen engages in interactive internet media such as games, chat rooms, and instant messaging, encourage her/him to make good decisions about what she/he posts and the amount of time she/he spends on these activities.
- Respect your teen's opinion. Listen to her/him without playing down her/his concerns.
- Encourage your teen to get enough sleep and exercise, and to eat healthy, balanced meals.
- Respect your teen's need for privacy.
- Encourage your teen to develop solutions to problems or conflicts. Help your teenager learn to make good decisions. Create opportunities for him to use his/her own judgment, and be available for advice and support.
- Talk with your teen about her concerns and pay attention to any changes in her behaviour. Ask him/her if he/she seems sad or depressed.
- Show interest in your teen's school and extracurricular interests and activities and encourage him to become involved in activities such as sports, music, theater and art.
- Encourage your teen to volunteer and become involved in civic activities in her community.

- Talk with your teen and help him plan ahead for difficult or uncomfortable situations. Discuss what he/she can do if he/she is in a group and someone is using drugs or under pressure to have sex, or is offered a ride by someone who has been drinking.
- Show affection for your teen. Spend time together doing things you enjoy.

CHAPTER 43 Adolescent Stages of Development

ADOLESCENCE: The Last stage of teen development before becoming an adult

Parents learn much about taking care of their babies and young children. Children pass through several stages of development or take specific steps, on their road to becoming adults. For most people, there are four or five such stages of growth where they learn certain things: infancy (birth to age two), early childhood (ages 3 to 8 years), later childhood (ages 9 to 12) and adolescence (ages 13 to 18). Persons 18 and over are considered adults in our society. We can say that everybody grows in this same pattern. It seems like everyone, even teachers and neighbours have problems understanding them. Giving up, you might turn to doing and saying the same things your parents did with you.

You can easily notice how it's right next to the adult stage, the last step before being an adult. This is a time for adolescents to decide about their future line of work. One of the first things they must do is to start making their own decisions. *For example*, adolescents can begin to decide what to buy with their pocket money. To do this they must put a little distance between themselves and their parents. This does not mean that parents can't continue to "look after them" or help them when needed.

You should, as much as possible, let them learn from the results of their actions. Adolescents also need to be around other adults, both male and female. These can be relatives, neighbours, or teachers. Of course, they have their role models. Adolescents can "spend hours" day dreaming about their future life. They might be planning the things they can do or will buy "when they grow up." Finally, don't worry if they want to spend time alone.

Adolescence: Period of changes and Developments

Adolescence is a transitional stage of physical and psychological human development that generally occurs during the period from puberty to adulthood The period of adolescence is most closely associated with the teenage years.

Within all of the perspectives of Psychology, Biology, History, Sociology, education and anthropology adolescence is viewed as a transitional period between childhood and adulthood. It is a period of multiple transitions involving education, training, employment and unemployment, as well as transitions from one living circumstance to another.

The end of adolescence and the beginning of adulthood varies by country and by function and furthermore even within a single nation state or culture there can be different ages at which an individual is considered mature enough for society to entrust them with certain privileges and responsibilities. Such milestones include driving a vehicle, having legal sexual relations, serving in the armed forces or on a jury, purchasing and drinking alcohol, voting, entering into contracts, finishing certain levels of education and marriage. Adolescence is usually accompanied by an increased independence allowed by the parents and less supervision as compared to preadolescence.

In popular culture, adolescent characteristics are attributed to physical changes and what is called change of hormones. Adolescence can be defined biologically, as the physical transition marked by the onset of puberty and the termination of physical growth; cognitively, as changes in the ability to think abstractly and multi-dimensionally; or socially, as a period of preparation for adult roles. Major pubertal and biological changes include changes to the sex organs, height, weight and muscle mass, as well as major changes in brain structure and organization. Cognitive advances encompass both increases in knowledge and in the ability to think abstractly and to reason more effectively.

1. Biological development of adolescent

Puberty

Puberty is a period of several years in which rapid physical growth and psychological changes occur, culminating in sexual maturity. **The average onset of puberty is at 10 or 11 for girls and age 12 or 13 for boys.** Every person's individual timetable for puberty is influenced primarily by heredity, although environmental factors, such as diet and exercise, also exert some influence. These factors can also contribute to precocious and delayed puberty.

Some of the most important parts of pubertal development involve distinctive physiological changes in individuals' height, weight, body composition and circulatory and respiratory systems. These changes are largely influenced by hormonal activity. Hormones play an organizational role, priming the body to behave in a certain way once puberty begins and an activational role, referring to changes in hormones during adolescence that trigger behavioral and physical changes.

Puberty occurs through a long process and begins with a **surge in hormone production**, which in turn causes a number of physical changes. It is the stage of life in which a child develops secondary sex characteristics. **Boys develop deeper voice and girls have development of breasts and more curved and prominent hips as his or her hormonal balance shifts strongly towards an adult state.** This is triggered by the pituitary gland, which secretes a surge of hormonal agents into the blood stream, initiating a chain reaction. The male and female hormones are subsequently activated, which puts them into a state of rapid growth and development. The triggered gonads now commence the mass production of the necessary chemicals. The testes primarily release testosterone, and the ovaries predominantly dispense estrogens. The production of these hormones increases gradually until sexual maturation is met.

Facial hair in males normally appears in a specific order during puberty: The first facial hair to appear tends to grow at the corners of the upper lip, typically between 14 to 17 years of age. It then spreads to form a moustache over the entire upper lip. This is followed by the appearance of hair on the upper part of the cheeks and the area under the lower lip. The hair eventually spreads to the sides and lower border of the chin and the rest of the lower face to form a full beard.

The major landmark of puberty for males is the first ejaculation, which occurs, on average, at age 13. For females, it is menarche, the onset of menstruation, which occurs, on average, between ages 12 and 13. The age of menarche is influenced by heredity, as well as girl's diet and lifestyle. Girls who have a high-fat diet and who are not physically active begin menstruating earlier.

For girls, early maturation can sometimes lead to increased self-consciousness. Because of their bodies' developing in advance, pubescent girls can become more insecure. Consequently, girls that reach sexual maturation early are more likely than their peers to develop eating disorders. Early maturing girls are more exposed to alcohol and drug abuse in big cities. Those who have had such experiences tend to perform less well in school than their "inexperienced" age peers.

Girls have usually reached full physical development by ages 15–17, while boys usually complete puberty by ages 16–17. Any increase in height beyond the post-pubertal age is uncommon. Girls attain reproductive maturity about 4 years after the first physical changes of puberty appear. In contrast, boys accelerate more slowly but continue to grow for about 6 years after the first visible pubertal changes.

The adolescent growth spurt is a **rapid increase in the individual's height and weight during puberty** resulting from the simultaneous release of growth hormones, thyroid hormones and androgens. Males experience their growth spurt about two years later, on average, than females. During their peak height velocity (the time of most rapid growth), adolescents grow at a growth rate nearly identical to that of a toddler—about 4 inches (10.3 cm) a year for males and 3.5 inches (9 cm) for females. In addition to changes in height, adolescents also experience a significant increase in weight. The weight gained during adolescence constitutes nearly half of one's adult body weight. Teenage and early adult males may continue to gain natural muscle growth even after puberty.

The accelerated growth in different body parts happens at different times, but for all adolescents it has a fairly regular sequence. The first places to grow are the extremities—the head, hands and feet—followed by the arms and legs, then the torso and shoulders. This non-uniform growth is one reason why an adolescent body may seem out of proportion.

During puberty, bones become **harder and more brittle**. At the conclusion of puberty, the ends of the long bones close during the process called epiphysis. There can be ethnic differences in these skeletal changes.

Another set of significant physical changes during puberty happen in bodily distribution of fat and muscle. This process is different for females and males. Before puberty, there are nearly no sex differences in fat and muscle distribution; during puberty, boys grow muscle much faster than girls, although both sexes experience rapid muscle development. In contrast, though both sexes experience an increase in body fat, the increase much more significant for girls. Frequently, the increase in fat for girls happens in their years just before puberty. The ratio between muscle and fat among post-pubertal boys is around three to one, while for girls it is about five to four. This may help explain sex differences in athletic performance.

Pubertal development also affects circulatory and respiratory systems as an adolescents' heart and lungs increase in both size and capacity. These changes lead to increased strength and tolerance for exercise. Sex differences are apparent as males tend to develop "larger hearts and lungs, higher systolic blood pressure, a lower resting heart rate, a greater capacity for carrying oxygen to the blood, a greater power for neutralizing the chemical products of muscular exercise, higher blood hemoglobin and more red blood cells".

Despite some genetic sex differences, environmental factors play a large role in biological changes during adolescence. *For example*, girls tend to reduce their physical activity in preadolescence and may receive inadequate nutrition from diets that often lack important nutrients, such as iron. These environmental influences in turn affect female physical development.

2. Reproduction-related developments in Boys and Girls

In males, these changes involve appearance of pubic, facial and body hair, deepening of the voice, roughening of the skin around the upper arms and thighs, and increased development of the sweat glands. In females, secondary sex changes involve elevation of the breasts, widening of the hips, development of pubic and underarm hair, widening of the areolae and elevation of the nipples.

3. Changes in the brain

The human brain is not fully developed by the time a person reaches puberty. **Between the ages of 10 and 25, the brain undergoes changes** that have important implications for behaviour. The brain reaches 90% of its adult size by the time a person is six years of age. Thus, the brain does not grow in size much during adolescence. However, the creases in the brain continue to become more complex until the late teens.

4. Cognitive Development

Adolescence is also a time for rapid cognitive development. Adolescence is the stage of life in which the individual's thoughts start taking more of an abstract form and the egocentric thoughts decrease. This allows the individual to think and reason in a wider perspective. The thoughts, ideas and concepts developed at this period of life greatly influence one's future life, playing a major role in character and personality formation.

Biological changes in brain structure and connectivity within the brain interact with increased experience, knowledge and changing social demands to produce rapid cognitive growth. The age at which particular changes take place varies between individuals.

Improvements in cognitive ability

By the time individuals have reached age 15 or so, their basic thinking abilities are comparable to those of adults. These **improvements occur in five areas during adolescence:**

1. **Attention:** Improvements are seen in selective attention, the process by which one focuses on one stimulus while tuning out another. Divided attention, the ability to pay attention to two or more stimuli at the same time, also improves.
2. **Memory**: Improvements are seen in both working memory and long-term memory.
3. **Processing speed:** Adolescents think more quickly than children. Processing speed improves sharply between age five and middle adolescence; it then begins to level off at age 15 and does not appear to change between late adolescence and adulthood.
4. **Organization:** Adolescents are more aware of their own thought processes and can use other strategies to think more efficiently.
5. **Metacognition:** A third gain in cognitive ability involves thinking about thinking itself, a process referred to as metacognition. It often involves monitoring one's own cognitive activity during the thinking process. Adolescents' improvements in knowledge of their own thinking patterns lead to better self-control and more effective studying. It is also relevant in social cognition, resulting in increased

introspection, self-consciousness and intellectualization. Adolescents are much better able than children to understand that people do not have complete control over their mental activity. The imaginary audience and the personal fable are likely peak at age fifteen, alongwith self-consciousness in general.

5. Social development and Identity development

The environment in which an adolescent grows up also plays an important role in their identity development. A common belief about adolescence is that it is the time when teenagers form personal identities. Three general approaches are used to understanding identity development: Self-concept, sense of identity, and self-esteem. The years of adolescence create a more conscientious group of young adults. Adolescents pay close attention and give more time and effort to their appearance as their body goes through changes. Unlike children, teens put forth an effort to look presentable..

6. Self-awareness

Early in adolescence, cognitive developments result in greater self-awareness, greater awareness of others and their thoughts and judgments, the ability to think about abstract, future possibilities, and the ability to consider multiple possibilities at once.

7. Relationship with Peers

The relationships with their peers, family and members of their social sphere play a vital role in the social development of an adolescent. As an adolescent's social sphere develops rapidly as they distinguish the differences between friends and acquaintances. They often become more emotionally involved in friends. This is not harmful; however, if these friends expose an individual to potentially harmful situations, this is an aspect of peer pressure. Adolescence is a vital period in social development because Adolescents can be easily influenced by the people they develop close relationships with. This is the first time individuals can truly make their own decisions.

Peer **groups are essential** to **social and general** development. Peer groups are especially important during adolescence, a period of development characterized by a dramatic increase in time spent with peers and a decrease in adult supervision. **Adolescents also associate with friends of the opposite much more than in childhood** and tend to identify with larger groups of peers based on shared characteristics. It is also common for adolescents to use friends as coping devices in different situations. High quality friendships may enhance children's development regardless of the characteristics of those friends. Susceptibility to peer pressure increases during early adolescence.

Peer groups offer members the opportunity to develop social skills such as empathy, sharing and leadership. **Peer groups can have positive influences on an individual**, such as on academic motivation and performance. But they can also have negative influences, like encouraging experimentation with drugs, drinking, vandalism, and stealing through peer pressure.

Romantic relationships tend to increase in prevalence throughout adolescence. Adolescence marks a time of sexual maturation, which manifests in social interactions as well. Kissing, hand holding and hugging signify satisfaction and commitment.

6. Relationship with the Family

When children go through puberty, **there is often a significant increase in parent-child conflict** and a less cohesive familial bond. Arguments often concern minor issues of control, such as **curfew**, acceptable clothing and the adolescent's right to privacy, which adolescents may have previously viewed as issues over which their parents had complete authority. Parent-adolescent disagreement also increases as friends demonstrate a greater impact on one another, new influences on the adolescent that may be in opposition to parents' values. Regarding their important life issues, most adolescents still share the same attitudes and values as their parents.

Siblings are a source of conflict and frustration as well as a support system during childhood. Adolescence may affect this relationship differently, depending on sibling gender. In same-sex sibling pairs, intimacy increases during early adolescence, then remains stable. Mixed-sex siblings pairs act differently; siblings drift apart during early adolescent years, but experience an increase in intimacy starting at middle adolescence.

Adolescents who have a good relationship with their parents are less likely to engage in various risk behaviours, such as smoking, drinking, fighting, and/or unprotected sexual intercourse. In addition, parents influence the education of adolescence. Despite changing family roles during adolescence, the home environment and parents are still important for the behaviours and choices of adolescents.

Stages of Adolescence

Adolescence, these years from puberty to adulthood, may be roughly divided into three stages: Early adolescence, generally ages eleven to fourteen; middle adolescence, ages fifteen to seventeen; and late adolescence, ages eighteen to twenty-one. In addition to physiological growth, seven key intellectual, psychological and social developmental tasks are squeezed into these years. The fundamental purpose of these tasks is to form one's own identity and to prepare for adulthood.

Stages of Adolescent Development

Stages of	Physical Development	Cognitive Development	Social-Emotional Development
Early Adolescence	• Puberty: Gro body hair, increase perspiration and oil production in hair and skin,	• Growing capacity for abstract thought • Mostly interested in present with limited thought to the	• Struggle with sense of identify • Feel awkward about one self and one's body, worry about being normal
Approximately 11—13 years of age	Girls–breast and hip development, onset of menstruation	• Intellectual interests expand become more important	• Realize that parents are not perfect, increased conflict with parents
	Boys–growth in testicles and penis, wet dreams, deepening of voice • Tremendous physical growth: gain height and weight • Greater sexual interest	• Deeper moral thinking	• increased influence of peer group • Desire for independence • Tendency to return to "childish" behaviour, particularly when stressed • Moodiness

			• Rule- and limit-testing • Greater interest in privacy
Middle Approximately 14–18 years of age	• Puberty is completed • Physical growth slows for girls, continues for boys	• Continued growth of capacity for abstract thought • Greater capacity for settings goals • Interest in moral reasoning • Thinking about the meaning	• Intense self-involvement, changing between high expectations and poor self-concept. • Continued adjustment to changing worries about being normal • Tendency to distantace selves from parents, continued drive for independecnce • Driven to make friends and greater reliance on them, popularity can be an important issue • Feelings of love and passion.

Late adolescence	• Young women, typically, are fully developed	• Ability to think ideas through • Ability to delay gratification	• Firmer sense of identify • Increased emotional stability
Approximately 19–21 years of age	• Young men continue to gain height, weight, muscle mass, and body hair	• Examination of inner experience • Increased concern for future • Continued interest in moral reasoning	• Increased concern for others • Increased independence and self-reliance • Peer relationships remain important • Development of more serious relationships • Social and cultural traditions regain some of their importance

CHAPTER

44 Realizing the Difference between Normal and Abnormal

You often think what the meaning is when we use the term "normal?" For the most part, children all over the world develop in much the same way. Babies quickly become attached to their parents or caregivers; begin to sit up at around six months. They start to walk right around their first birthdays. From the earliest days after birth when its seem like all they can really do is cry, sleep and eat. The rapid change that happens during the first two years of life is amazing.

Being a parent you will be watching with anticipation as your child reaches each of these developmental milestones. Sometimes you will be worrying if your child does not reach these milestones as quickly as other children of his or her age group. This is perhaps one of the greatest reasons to learn as much as you can about child development. If you know what is supposed to be happening and when it's supposed to happen, you will be able to recognize if your child's growth is not proceeding as it should.

Understanding normal development of a child can also help ease worries or fears of parents. While children tend to follow the same developmental progression, it is very important to understand that not all children achieve the same things at exactly the same ages. While your friend's son or daughter was walking by eleven months or so, it may take your own daughter 12 or 13 months or a bit more time to reach that same point. Realizing that individual differences are also part of normal development can help put your mind at ease.

When a child falls far behind his or her peers or fails to achieve these basic milestones, obtaining outside assessment from professionals is important. By seeking help early, parents can ensure that their children get the help they need to grow and thrive.

When development does not follow a normal path, it is often referred to as abnormal development. It is important to remember that in many cases, it may involve things that are not particularly abnormal. Learning disabilities, emotional disorders and behavioural problems can all present very real challenges, but these impairments do not mean that a child is "abnormal." In some cases, developmental problems may be a result of environmental changes. Death, divorce, and traumatic events can cause children to experience mood changes, anxiety and misbehaviour.

As we learn more about child psychology and development, we should try to avoid creating normal and abnormal categorizations of what's normal and what's not. It is essential to remember that each child is a unique individual full of a distinctive blend of traits, abilities, and experiences. So make sure that your child may be different from others, and then there is no need to worry.

By understanding both normal and abnormal development parents, teachers and doctors are better able to keep an eye out for potential problems. This is important because early detection results in early intervention. The sooner a child receives help with a developmental problem, the better outcome is likely to be. The greater improvement the child is likely to demonstrate at an early stage.

Problems with Physical Development

You often focus on developmental issues related to psychological or behaviour issues, physical problems can also impede normal development. In addition to chronic illness, children can be born with birth defects that can seriously impact their ability to function and achieve physical milestones of development.

Some of these physical problems may be present at birth, but some may only become evident as the child matures. Parents should be on the alert for potential issues that might make crawling, walking, sleeping, or eating difficult for them.

Problems with Learning Development

Learning plays a major role in the life of a child. From the earliest days of a child's life, he is undergoing a continual process of learning. This learning will have a dramatic impact, affecting how the child things, feels, and behaves. School is the most obvious example of this; learning does not just take place in academic settings.

Learning is one of the most important parts of child development, which is why it is essential for parents and teachers to know how to spot potential learning problems. Attention problem and learning disabilities can make it difficult for a child to focus and perform well academically. But identifying these problems early and responding with appropriate interventions makes it possible for kids to overcome such issues and achieve their full potential.

Parents and teachers must be alert and knowledgeable about what to look for. Sometimes such issues can be easy to spot. Poor attention, delayed speech and late motor skill development are all possible signs of a learning problem.

Learning disabilities are a group of neurological disorders which become evident in childhood. These disabilities are characterized by difficulty in learning, sorting and storing information. Children with learning disabilities may have one or more difficulties with skills such as listening, speaking, reading, writing, reasoning, or mathematical abilities that interfere with academic performance, achievement. In some cases these disabilities interfere with the activities of daily living. Learning disabilities may overlap with other disorders or environmental influences, but are not the direct result of those conditions or influences.

Often these disabilities are not identified until a child reaches school age. Performances on standardized tests are usually found to be below that expected for age. Standardized cognitive measures and diagnostic tools in addition to observations from education professionals help to identify areas where these children are experiencing problems.

Some children find learning in a regular classroom difficult and learning disability classes may be recommended to help them receive more specific and intensive teaching. Generally Learning disabilities are life long, but with proper intervention, training, and strategies, individuals can lead successful, fully functioning lives. Sometimes they become so perfect adult that it is difficult to find their problem easily.

CHAPTER 45 Common Behavioural Problems in Children

Behavioural disorders may be caused by a number of factors such as parenting style which is inconsistent or contradictory, family or marital problems, child abuse or neglect, overindulgence, injury or chronic illness, separation or bereavement. Children do not always display their reactions to events immediately, although they may emerge later. Anticipatory guidance can be helpful to parents and children . The parents can attempt to prepare children in advance of any potentially traumatic events such as Separation. Children should be allowed to express their true fears and anxieties about impending events.

The child's problems are often multi-factorial and the way in which they are expressed may be influenced by a range of factors including developmental stage, temperament, coping and adaptive abilities of family, and the nature and the duration of stress.

Many behaviours, which are probably undesirable but a normal occurrence at an early stage of development, can be considered disruptive behaviour when they present at a later age.

It can be difficult to assess whether the behaviour of such children is normal or sufficiently problematical to require intervention. Judgement will need to take into account the frequency, range and intensity of symptoms and the extent to which they cause impairment. Behaviour problems can be due to many disorders. These can be usefully classified into various disorders

- **Psychosocial disorders**
- **Habit disorders**
- **Anxiety disorders**
- **Disruptive behaviour**
- **Sleeping problems**

Psychosocial disorders

These may manifest as disturbance in:

- **Emotions:** *for example*, anxiety or depression.
- **Behaviour:** *for example*, aggression.
- **Physical function:** *for example*, psychogenic disorders.
- **Mental performance:** *for example*, problems at school.

In stressful situations, young children will tend to react with impaired physiological functions such as feeding and sleeping disturbances. Older children may exhibit relationship disturbances with friends and family, poor school performance, behavioural regression to an earlier developmental stage and development of specific psychological disorders such as phobia or psychosomatic illness. .

Habit Disorders

These include a range of phenomena that may be described as Behaviour Problems

Thumb sucking	Repetitive vocalisations	Tics
Nail biting	Hair pulling	Breath holding
Air swallowing	Head banging	
Body rocking	Manipulating parts of the body	Hitting or biting themselves

All children will at some developmental stage display repetitive behaviours but whether they may be considered as disorders depends on their frequency and persistence and the effect they have on physical, emotional and social functioning. These habit behaviours may arise originally from intentional movements which become repeated and then become incorporated into the child's customary behaviour. Some habits arise in imitation of adult behaviour. Other habits such as hair pulling or head banging develop as a means of providing a form of sensory input and comfort when the child is alone.

The most common disruptive behaviour disorders in children include **Oppositional Defiant Disorder (ODD), Conduct Disorder (CD) and Attention Deficit Hyperactivity Disorder (ADHD)**. Treatment can include therapy, education and medication.

All young children can be naughty, defiant and impulsive from time to time, which is perfectly normal. However, some children have extremely difficult and challenging behaviours that are outside the norm for their age.

Thumb sucking

This is quite normal in early infancy. If it continues, it may interfere with the alignment of developing teeth. It is comfort behaviour of infants and parents should try to ignore it while providing encouragement and reassurance about other aspects of the child's activities.

Tics

These are repetitive movements of muscle groups that reduce tension arising from physical and emotional states, involving the head, the neck and hands most frequently. It is difficult for the child with a tic to inhibit it for more than a short period. Parental pressure may exacerbate it, while ignoring the tic can reduce it. Tics can be differentiated by their absence during sleep.

Stuttering

This is not a tension-reducing habit. It arises in 5% of children as they learn to speak. About 20% of these retain the stuttering into adulthood. It is more prevalent in boys than in girls. Initially, it is better to ignore the problem since most cases will resolve spontaneously. If the disfluency in speech persists and is causing concern , you should consult to a speech therapist.

Anxiety and Fearfulness

Anxiety and fearfulness are part of normal development. However, if they persist and become generalised, they can develop into socially disabling conditions and require intervention. Approximately 6-7% of children may develop anxiety disorders and, of these, 1/3 may be over-anxious while 1/3 may have some phobia. Anxiety disorder, social phobia, separation anxiety disorder, obsessive-compulsive disorder and phobia are demonstrated by a diffuse or specific anxiety predictably caused by certain situations.

School phobia occurs in many of children and there is a strong association with anxiety and depression. Management is by treating the underlying psychiatric condition, family therapy, parental training and liaison with the school in order to investigate possible reasons for refusal and negotiate re-entry.

Breathlessness and Temper Tantrums

In the young child, many behaviours such as breath holding or temper tantrums are probably the result of anger and frustration at their inability to control their own environment. For some of these situations it is wise for parents to avoid a punitive response and, if possible, to remove themselves from the room. It is quite likely that the child will be frightened by the intensity of their own behaviour and will need comfort and reassurance.

While some isolated incidents of stealing or lying are normal occurrences of early development, they may warrant intervention if they persist. Truancy, arson, antisocial behaviour and aggression should not be considered as normal developmental features.

Attention deficit hyperactivity disorder

It is characterised by poor ability to attend to tasks *for example*, child makes careless mistakes, avoids sustained mental effort, motor over activity and impulsiveness as the child blurts out answers, interrupts others. Behavioural modification and neuro-feedback are the non-pharmacological treatments with the largest evidence base. Various dietary interventions have been mooted.

Sleeping Problems

Sleep disorders can be defined as more or less sleep than is appropriate for the age of the child. By the age of 1-3 months, the longest daily sleep should bein the night. Sleeping through the night is a developmental milestone but, at the age of 1 year, 30% of children may still be waking in the night. Stable sleep patterns may not be present until age 5 years but parental or environmental factors can encourage the development of circadian rhythm.

Most kids will display behaviour that will either edify or embarrass parents at some stage of their school lives.

Oppositional Defiant Disorder

Around one in ten children under the age of 12 years are thought to have **Oppositional Defiant Disorder (ODD)**, with boys outnumbering girls by two to one. Here are some of the typical behaviours of a child with ODD .

- Child refuses to obey rules
- Child is easily angered, annoyed or irritated
- Child seems to deliberately try to annoy or aggravate others
- Child seeks to blame others for any misfortunes or misdeeds.
- Child shows frequent temper tantrums
- Child argues frequently with adults, particularly the most familiar adults in their lives, such as parents
- Child seems to deliberately try to annoy or aggravate others
- Child has low self-esteem

Conduct Problem

Children with Conduct Disorder (CD) are often judged as 'bad kids' because of their delinquent behaviour and refusal to accept rules. Around five percent of 10 year olds are thought to have CD, with boys outnumbering girls by four to one. Around one-third of children with CD also have Attention Deficit Hyperactivity Disorder (ADHD).

Some of the typical behaviours of a child with CD may include:

- Frequent lying
- Lack of empathy for others
- Frequent refusal to obey parents or other authority figures
- Tendency to use drugs, including cigarettes and alcohol, at a very early age
- Being aggressive to animals and other people or showing sadistic behaviours including bullying and physical or sexual abuse
- Keenness to start physical fights
- Using weapons in physical fights
- Criminal behaviour such as stealing, deliberately lighting fires, breaking into houses and vandalism
- A tendency to run away from home

Attention deficit hyperactivity disorder

Around two to five per cent of children are thought to have Attention Deficit Hyperactivity Disorder (ADHD), with boys outnumbering girls by three to one. The characteristics of ADHD can include:

- **Inattention**: Difficulty concentrating, forgetting instructions, moving from one task to another without completing anything.

- **Impulsivity:** Talking over the top of others, having a 'short fuse', being accident-prone.
- **Over activity:** Constant restlessness and fidgeting.
- **Intellectual disabilities:** Children with intellectual disabilities are twice as likely to have behavioural disorders.
- **Brain development:** Studies have shown that areas of the brain that control attention appear to be less active in children with ADHD.

OTHER BEHAVIOUR DISORDERS AND PROBLEMS

Dyslexia

Dyslexia is a learning disorder in which children have delayed language development, trouble with rhyming words, hesitation, mispronunciation and word finding difficulties. It is one of the most common learning disorders.

Dyslexia is a persistent chronic disorder and not a transient development lag. It is both heritable and familial. Many parents of dyslexic children have themselves been suffering from this disorder.

Dyslexic children have difficulty in learning alphabets, number and association of sound with letters. They read very slowly, inaccurate and difficultly. Many times they reverse the letters. Their spellings are incorrect and poor.

Solution

Special teaching and reading programmes are designed for dyslexic children. Parent or teacher has to involve more actively in teaching such children. Computers with spelling check programmes, tape recorders and recorded books can be helpful for these children. Examination can administered orally in place of writing examination. These changes can help dyslexic children to grow properly with the progress of other common children.

Periodic Syndrome

Some children show certain problem symptoms periodically like headache, diarrhoea, stomach pain, body pain, constipation and breathlessness. These symptoms occur at various times and at various combinations. They're occur over a period of weeks or months. Between these symptoms or attacks, child is quite normal.

Tense family atmosphere, avoidance of any work or school, school pressure, fear of any teacher and many other stressful factors may be the root cause of these problems.

Solution

Investigation by the parents is very necessary. Usually all investigations are found normal and there is no evidence of infection. So no medical treatment is required.

Assurance and assistance of parents is the best solutions. Parents may try to reduce stress in the family and burden of the school.

Pica

Pica is a problem in which child eats those substances which are not supposed to be eaten like dust, soil, sand, plaster of walls, chalk, clay, flakes of paints, pieces of bricks, pieces or corners of planters, fabrics etc. It is very common problem in the children below two years and may rarely continue till later in life.

Parents generally try to stop or sometimes ignore below the two years child. Pica does not need any treatment in the absence of associated organic problem. Pica usually occurs in children with history of poor parental attention, neglect, poor supervision, dependence on maid. Such children are often anaemic with minerals, calcium and vitamin deficiency. These children may have worm infection in their stomach.

Solution

Persistence of pica needs medical attention. Doctors may prescribe iron, vitamin or minerals and de- worming medicines. Parents' proper attention and check is required to stop this problem.

Things to remember

- Boys are more likely than girls to suffer from behavioural disorders.
- Treatment options include parent management training, cognitive behaviour therapy, medication and treatment for associated problems.
- Some children have extremely difficult and challenging behaviours that are outside the norm for their age.

These problems can result from temporary stressors in the child's life, or they might represent more enduring disorders. The most common disruptive behaviour disorders include **Oppositional Defiant Disorder (ODD), Conduct Disorder (CD) and Attention Deficit Hyperactivity Disorder (ADHD).**

CHAPTER 46 Right Age for Bowel and Bladder Training

Almost all children have wetting or soiling accidents at one time or another. As with other models of developmental milestones, transient regressions or delays in toilet training logically can be expected. Bowel maturation typically precedes bladder maturation, which is not surprising, given the respective complexities of the developmental processes. An estimated 15% to 20% of children will become partially toilet trained but continue to have wetting accidents after age 5. Additionally, at least 15-20% of developmentally normal children 18 to 30 months of age may refuse stool toilet training at one point.

Toilet-Training

Toilet-training is teaching your child to recognize his or her body signals for urinating and having a bowel movement and using a potty chair or toilet correctly and at the appropriate times.

Time to begin Training

Toilet-training should begin when the child shows signs that he or she is ready. There is no right age to begin. If you try to toilet train before your child is ready, it can be a battle for both mother and child. The ability to control bowel and bladder muscles comes with proper growth and development.

Children develop at different rates. A child younger than 12 months of age has no control over bladder or bowel movements. There is very little control between 12 to 18 months. Most children are unable to obtain bowel and bladder control until 24 to 30 months. It is assumed that the average age of toilet-training is 27 months.

Indications

The following may be indicators of your child's readiness to begin toilet-training. Your child should be able to:

1. Tell you when there is a need to go to the potty.
2. Walk well in order to get to the potty chair.
3. Control the muscles used for going to the potty.
4. Shows discomfort when the diaper is wet or dirty
5. Asks to have the diaper changed or tells you a bowel movement or urine is coming
6. Has dry diapers for at least two hours during the day or is dry after naps or overnight
7. Enjoys copying what parents or older children do
8. Follows you into the bathroom and see how the toilet is used
9. Wants to do things (like going to the potty) to make parents happy or to get praise

When Not to Start Potty/Toilet Training

There are some issues that can sometimes get in the way of successful potty training. *For example*, when children are going through a significant change or several changes at once it might be smart to hold off on adventures in potty training. At these times, children often feel overwhelmed and sometimes lose skills they have already learned or were making progress on, like potty training. Common situations that can cause stress and are generally not good times to start training include:

- An upcoming or recent family move.
- Beginning new or changing existing child care arrangements.
- Switching from crib to bed.
- When you are expecting or have recently had a new baby.
- A major illness, a recent death, or some other family crisis.

If your child is in the middle of potty training during a stressful time and seems to be having more accidents than usual, know that this is normal. Your child needs all of your patience and support right now. She will return to her previous level of potty training once things have gotten back to normal.

Tips for easy start for toilet-training:

- The following tips may help parents get started with toilet-training: It is best to use a potty chair on the floor rather than putting the child on the toilet for training. The potty chair is more secure for most children because their feet reach the floor and there is no fear of falling off. If you decide to use a seat that goes over the toilet, use a footrest for your child's feet.
- If there are siblings, ask them to let the younger child see you praising them for using the toilet.
- Children should be allowed to play with the potty: Sit on it with clothes on and later with diapers off. This way they can get used to it.
- Your child should not sit on the potty for more than five minutes. Sometimes, children have a bowel movement just after the diaper is back on because the diaper feels normal. Do not get upset or punish your child. You can try taking the dirty diaper off and putting the bowel movement in the potty with your child watching you. This may help your child understand that you want the bowel movement in the potty.
- Never strap your child to the potty chair. Children should be free to get off the potty when they want.
- Children often learn to go to the potty for bowel movements before urine, so you may want to start with bowel training first.
- If your child has a usual time for bowel movements (such as after a meal) you can take your child to the potty at that time of day. If your child acts a certain way when having a bowel movement (such as stooping, getting quiet, going to the

corner), you may try taking your child to potty when he or she shows it is time.

- If your child wants to sit on the potty, you may stay next to your child and talk and read a book.
- It is good to use words for what your child is doing ("potty," or "poop"). Then your child learns the words to tell you. Remember that other people will hear these words. It is best not to use words that will offend, confuse, or embarrass others or your child.
- Avoid using words like "dirty," "naughty," or "stinky" to describe bowel movements and urine. Use a simple, matter-of-fact tone.
- Some children learn by pretending to teach a doll to go potty. Obtain a doll that has a hole in mouth and diaper area and your child can feed and "teach" the doll to pull down pants and use the potty. Make this teaching fun for your child.
- Make going to the potty a part of your child's daily routine, such as first thing in the morning, after meals and naps and before going to bed.
- If your child gets off the potty before urinating or passing a bowel movement, be calm; do not scold. Try again later. If your child successfully uses the potty, give plenty of praise (i.e., smile, clap, hug).
- Children learn from copying adults and other children. It may help if your child sits on the potty while you are using the toilet.
- Children often follow parents into the bathroom. This may be one time they are willing to use the potty.
- Initially, teach boys to sit down for passing urine, as, at first, it is difficult to control starting and stopping while standing. Boys will try to stand to urinate when they see other boys standing.

• • •

Other Books on

GENERAL BOOKS

1. The Art of Personality Development **(New)**	150/-
2. Think & Grow Rich **(New)**	150/-
3. Abraham Lincoln : A Complete Biography **(New)**	195/-
4. Mein Kampf : My Struggle **(New)**	195/-
5. Child Development (New)	195/-
6. Positive Mind Power (New)	150/-
7. Travel & Tourism An Industry Facilitator (New)	295/-
8. World's Great Authors And Poets (New)	125/-
9. Judgment No Aircrash No Death (New)	250/-
10. Effective Editing Help Yourself in Becoming A Good Editor (New)	125/-
11. Smart House-Keeping for Modern Women	125/-
12. Develop Super Power Memory	125/-
13. World's Great Personalities	125/-
14. Personality Plus	125/-
15. Power of Positive Thinking	125/-
16. Art of Successful Parenting	150/-
17. A Handbook of Etiquettes	125/-
18. How to Beat Your Competitors	125/-
19. How to Negotiate Effectively	125/-
20. World's Great Scientists	125/-
21. Patriot The Unique Indian Leader Netaji Subhas Chandra Bose	250/-
22. Body Language	125/-
23. Art of Successful Living	125/-
24. Make Your Boss Happy	125/-

25. Jokes for All	110/-
26. Selected Dohas	295/-
27. Baby Names for Girls (New)	95/-
28. Baby Names for Boys (New)	95/-
29. Art of Public Speaking	125/-
30. The World's Greatest Speeches	125/-
31. Group Discussions	110/-
32. Personality Development	95/-
33. Think Positive & Things Will Go Right	95/-
34. Once in a Blue Moon (A Tantra Tale)	125/-
35. God is Dead	125/-
36. Travel India (A Complete Guide For Tourists)	295/-
37. Glimpses of Urdu Poetry	350/-
38. Indian Mythology	195/-
39. Helpline for Stressed Parents	125/-
40. Grow Rich with Peace of Mind	125/-
41. How to be Fit & Young (New)	125/-
42. How to Succeed in Life	125/-
43. How to Reduce Tension	125/-
44. A Book of Stenography	150/-
45. Business Letters	110/-
46. Baby Names for the Boy	85/-
47. Baby Names for the Girl	85/-
48. Non Vegetarian Delights	110/-
49. Pure Vegetarian Delights	110/-